Praise for *The Entrepreneurial Conversation*

The Entrepreneurial Conversation provides a clear, engaging and convincing guide to building mutually beneficial relationships. Through practical examples, the authors explain what constitutes an entrepreneurial mindset. Readers of different professions will benefit greatly from reading this enjoyable book.

> *Kira S. Sheinerman, Ph.D.*
> *Vice President, Investment Banking*
> *Rodman & Renshaw, LLC*

After more than thirty years managing hundreds of salespeople and thousands of clients, I've read all sorts of books on selling and marketing, and they inevitably boil down to one thing: closing tactics. This book is different. Once you've mastered the true art of the "entrepreneurial conversation," you'll no longer be stressed out about getting the order. This book explains how "closing" can become the natural, predictable and comfortable outcome of mutually beneficial interactions with your customers.

> *Phil Zachary, Executive Vice President/COO*
> *Curtis Media Group*

The Entrepreneurial Conversation is not about tips, tricks and techniques for success, but how to train yourself to think, listen and speak effectively so success comes to you. *The Entrepreneurial Conversation* is simple and clear. It has been a tremendous help in establishing my business as a growing jewelry designer, manufacturer, and distributor.

> *Judith O'Dell, Founder, Studio CPU*

The Entrepreneurial Conversation shows that by focusing on the real issues of your clients and employees you can work to achieve both their and your success. By being other-oriented and not self-oriented, you can learn to develop mutually beneficial goals and relationships with clients, customers and employees.

> *Peter A. Arthur-Smith, Founding Principal,*
> *International Leadership Advisor,*
> *Modern Age Leadership/Leadership Solutions, Inc.*

The Entrepreneurial Conversation

The Powerful Way to Create Mutually Beneficial, Long-Term Business Relationships

Edward G. Rogoff & Michael Corbett
with Perry-Lynn Moffitt

For more information contact:
Pinnacle Books, Inc. • 877-249-4974
or visit www.theentrepreneurialconversation.com

Book design by Jack Mayer

Cover design by James Stagnitta

Printing number: 9 8 7 6 5 4 3 2
Printed in Canada

Rogoff, Edward G., 1951-

The entrepreneurial conversation : the powerful way to create mutually beneficial, long-term business relationships / by Edward G. Rogoff and Michael Corbett.

p. cm.
Includes index.
LCCN 2005926775
ISBN 0966738373

1. Relationship marketing. 2. Selling. 3. Entrepreneurship.
I. Corbett, Michael, 1942- II. Title.

HF5415.55.R65 2006   658.8'12   QBI05-600154

BK - ROTH
$ 14.95

Dedications

To my mother…
her wisdom is on every page.
E.G.R.

To Carole Savitt…
partner, mentor, wise and loving friend.
You are missed so much.
M.C.

Table of Contents

preface

You might consider us the typical odd couple. Edward Rogoff is a professor who wrote his Ph.D. dissertation under the supervision of Nobel Prize-winning economist William Vickery. Michael Corbett worked as a part-time radio announcer while serving in the Air Force. Once discharged, he worked full time in radio and eventually moved on to other endeavors.

Our paths crossed when Ed started his first broadcasting company and realized that selling in the radio business meant relying on out-of-date tricks designed to manipulate potential advertisers into parting with their money. By that time, Michael had developed his own sales training business based on his post-radio announcer years as a sales and marketing manager, advertising agency founder, and media executive. Michael knew exactly how to teach salespeople to move beyond the old bunk and become more effective in their jobs.

Ed hired Michael to present a seminar for both advertisers and salespeople at one of his fourteen radio stations. He stood in the back of the room and was captivated by what Michael had to say. Ed heard about a new kind of sales effectiveness based on having straightforward conversations that explored possibilities and built long-term, mutually beneficial relationships, rather than simply convincing someone to buy something once.

That was in 1985 and we have been working together ever since. Ed founded another broadcasting company and eventually returned to the academic world where he became an award-winning professor of business management at Baruch College in New York City. He authored the recently published *Bankable Business Plans*, and has written numerous articles about entrepreneurship and business. He has served several years as Director of the Field Center for Entrepreneurship, one of the largest business labs in the United States.

Michael wrote his best-selling book, *The 33 Ruthless Rules of Local Advertising*, and continues to work with hundreds of salespeople and business owners each year through his successful seminars on how to avoid old-school selling techniques by building long-term, mutually beneficial relationships between sellers and buyers.

In our combined careers of more than sixty years in business management, sales, training, education, and the establishment of our own successful entrepreneurial ventures, we have observed hundreds of people during thousands of interactions that were intended to further their personal and professional goals. We have read scores of books and dozens of studies about human relations, entrepreneurship, management, selling, and business growth.

After all this observation and analysis, we realized that the only thing that's ever going on during any interaction between people, whether it's a large-scale business meeting, a sales presentation, or a job interview, is thinking, listening and speaking.

We also discovered that the people who seemed to think, listen and speak most effectively were the many successful entrepreneurs we encountered over the years. We saw how successful entrepreneurs engage in conversations that further the process of starting and growing their own enterprises. They believe in a vision that propels them forward, they know how to motivate others to support their objectives, and they understand the value of building long-term relationships with their clients, investors and employees. Successful entrepreneurs know how to think, listen and speak so that others become enthusiastic participants in achieving their shared goals.

We call these effective dialogues *entrepreneurial conversations*.

As we explored the best way to teach others how to harness the power of an entrepreneurial conversation, we both realized that this concept of thinking, listening and speaking effectively applies not only to business but also to any mutually beneficial relationship, be it doctor and patient, artist and buyer, or research scientist and colleagues. It even applies to teachers communicating with their students and children relating to their parents. In fact, any ongoing relationship that is invested in a mutually beneficial, long-term outcome can profit from entrepreneurial conversations.

What you are about to read is the collaboration of this seemingly odd couple, whose varied skills, knowledge, backgrounds, and mutual respect led to our writing this book together. *The Entrepreneurial Conversation* shows you how to employ the art of thinking, listening and speaking so you can produce real and sometimes unexpected results in all of your business relationships. We also include two chapters on how the power of the entrepreneurial conversation can help managers and salespeople improve their effectiveness.

To illustrate our main points, each chapter concludes with a section called "Wisdom of the Entrepreneurial Masters," in-depth profiles of successful individuals we have encountered in a variety of fields who have taken thinking, listening and speaking to new heights. Most of our examples are based on business interactions, so we often refer to the people engaged in entrepreneurial conversations as investors, clients or employees, but be open-minded about applications of the entrepreneurial conversation. Clients are patients if you're a physician, students if you're a teacher, employees if you're a boss. Conversations, remember, are two-way streets.

Our book will not make you wake up feeling like a tiger, nor will it tell you how to memorize scripts or imitate experienced professionals. But it will show you how you can be yourself and master the art of the entrepreneurial conversation so you can develop long-term, productive relationships with anyone whose support and cooperation you seek. We urge you to return to this book often to refresh your knowledge of the entrepreneurial conversation. Pick a page at random and ask yourself if you have fully applied the lessons there.

The twenty years we have worked together developing the concepts of *The Entrepreneurial Conversation*, have been one of the most satisfying experiences of our professional lives. Teaching these principles to our clients and students, and seeing the results that followed, were the proof we needed that thinking, listening and speaking like a successful entrepreneur will help you achieve your goals. So take our advice; master the creative art of engaging in entrepreneurial conversations and you will be able to build even greater success for yourself in any endeavor.

Good luck, and may all of your conversations be entrepreneurial.

Edward G. Rogoff, New York, New York
Michael Corbett, Kingsland, Georgia

January 2005

acknowledgments by Edward G. Rogoff

When I first heard Michael Corbett speak more than twenty years ago, I knew I was hearing ideas that were uniquely his—and uniquely right. In the years that have followed, I have become a proselytizer for Michael's thinking. *The Entrepreneurial Conversation* is just one more step in that process. Working with Michael Corbett, being his friend, and continuing to learn from him has provided me with some of the richest experiences of my life.

This book—and all of my work—has gained immeasurably from my association with many wonderful colleagues. At Baruch College I am surrounded by an extraordinary group of scholars, including Professors Ramona K.Z. Heck, Robert Foskey, Myung-Soo Lee, Alvin N. Puryear and Harry Rosen.

Many of my professional colleagues have contributed significantly to this book, including Monica Dean, Carla Hojaiban, Basant Kedia, Rita Ormsby, Bill Parshall and Richard Rosenstein.

Tragically, just a few months before this book was published, my dear friend and colleague Neal

Welsh died. Neal epitomized the qualities of the entrepreneurial conversation. He made every interaction into a win-win situation. His unfailing ethical and professional standards earned him tremendous admiration and loyalty among his friends and colleagues. As I worked to explain the principles of an entrepreneurial conversation, I would often ask myself, "What would Neal do in this situation?" So Neal's spirit lives on every page of this book.

As her name on the cover shows, I have greatly benefited from being married to a wonderful writer and editor, Perry-Lynn Moffitt. The most challenging part of writing the book you are about to read was distilling and organizing the material to make it as clear, useful, and compelling as possible. The credit for this goes to her.

Mike Shatzkin, my friend and agent, has been essential to the process of creating this book. Mike's creativity, his incredible knowledge of publishing, and his enthusiasm for *The Entrepreneurial Conversation* have been indispensable.

acknowledgments by Michael Corbett

This book is based on sales training that my partner, Dave Stilli, and I conducted for co-author Ed Rogoff's former group of radio stations. An integral part of that training was how to communicate for success—how to manage the entrepreneurial conversation components of thinking, listening and speaking effectively so that much more was accomplished in a fraction of the normal time.

Ed and I remained friends after he sold his stations, and on a visit to my home, he suggested that we write a book on the subject. Ed's academic discipline allows him to write with a lot more patience than I can muster. Having written *The 33 Ruthless Rules of Local Advertising*, I told him I'd rather not tackle another writing project, but I said I'd do so if I could provide essential ideas based on my communications course, contextual guidance and some modest amounts of actual toil. He was to provide the research and other heavy lifting. He agreed (knowing he had his remarkable wife, Perry-Lynn Moffitt, to contribute), and that's how this book was launched.

In addition to Dave, Ed and Perry-Lynn, I would like to recognize others who are important to my work and, therefore, my life: my family, of course; Dave's family, who have made me a part of their own; Jack Mayer, whose talent has made *The Entrepreneurial Conversation* look beautiful and read smoothly; my clients, most of whom are media owners; and those managers and salespeople who understand the power of the entrepreneurial conversation.

I hope the wisdom in this book makes a difference in your business relationships. That is the only reason it was written.

1 the Power of the entrepreneurial conversation

The entrepreneurial conversation is a powerful way to think, listen and speak which builds mutually beneficial, long-term business relationships.

Why *Entrepreneurial*?

This is the age of entrepreneurship. Today businesses begin, grow and reorganize without missing a beat. People change careers and learn new skills in order to start and expand their own enterprises or establish their value to their employers. Large corporations, once considered the antithesis of entrepreneurial spirit, are adopting this faster-paced, more nimble approach to business.

This explosion of entrepreneurial behavior demands increased interaction with people, better communication skills, and a greater reliance on new sources of revenue. If we can express our needs and understand the needs of others effectively, then we will be able to build mutually beneficial, long-term relationships, and our endeavors will succeed.

The successful entrepreneurs we have encountered over the years are almost impossible to categorize. They come in all shapes and sizes. They have widely-diverse educational backgrounds and economic resources. Their success does not depend on gender, ethnicity, age, religion or political beliefs. It isn't necessarily measured in dollars earned or in the number of people they employ. Job satisfaction and independence, as well as the act of creating something of their own, are their primary ambitions.

In our combined careers of over sixty years as entrepreneurs, business consultants and educators, we have determined that successful entrepreneurs can be defined only by the crucial ability they all share: They know how to think, listen and speak effectively.

Successful entrepreneurs think up business ambitions based on their dreams. And they listen carefully to others so they can determine where mutual goals will intersect. They speak persuasively to gain support for their efforts. Being able to think, listen and speak effectively in a productive dialogue also enables successful entrepreneurs to grab opportunities, take risks and inspire others to work hard to achieve mutually beneficial long-term objectives.

> "If you will have tomorrow what others will not have, you must do today what others will not do."
> — *Anonymous*

Why *Conversation*?

We believe that the core force that drives each and every successful entrepreneurial enterprise is a conversation between people in which they reveal their needs, hopes, capabilities and personalities. These conversations determine whether further interaction will be mutually beneficial or the participants will go their own separate ways.

In spite of the current proliferation of electronic communication such as fax, e-mail and voice-messages, there is absolutely no interaction that is as dynamic or effective as a conversation. Many experts agree with us. According to noted business professor Alan Weber, conversations are the modern dynamo of business:

> Time was, if the boss caught you talking at the water cooler, he would have said, "Stop talking and get to work!" Today if you're not on the phone or talking with colleagues or customers, chances are you'll hear, "Start

talking and get to work!" In the new economy, conversations are the most important form of work. Conversations are the way knowledge workers discover what they know, share it with colleagues, and in the process create new knowledge for the organization. Conversations are the channel for learning what's really important to customers. Companies that practice the art of conversation are more apt to discern subtle changes in consumer taste, and are more likely to spread that new awareness rapidly through the organization; and by their fast response, be better positioned to shape the new environment to which slower competitors must then respond.

We want to make certain, however, that you understand the qualities of a truly effective conversation and the difference between a conversation and its polar opposite—a debate. In their book, *Dialogue: Rediscover the Transforming Power of Conversation*, Linda Ellinor and Glenna Gerard explain that when participants harden their positions, they begin to argue. They stop listening to one another and their conversation becomes a competition with a winner and a loser. As Ellinor and Gerard see it, our ability to move closer to dialogue and further away from debate leads us to meaningful, mutually beneficial results.

Psychologist William Isaacs of MIT's Sloan School of Management in his book *Dialogue: The Art of Thinking Together*, explains that a true conversation "invents unprecedented possibilities and new insights, and produces a collective flow," because the participants suspend their personal investment in fixed positions and explore all of the possibilities. A debate, he believes, is an attempt to beat down the other party and defend the position you brought to the conversation.

We call these ineffective dialogues *old-school conversations*. They fail because they focus on the differences between people and erect barriers between them. The entrepreneurial conversation, in contrast, focuses on the connections between people, enabling them to create mutually beneficial working relationships and make entrepreneurial conversations the main way they interact. In old-school-style communication, participants justify and defend their individual assumptions, while people engaged in entrepreneurial conversations question all the assumptions. In old-school conversations, each person attempts to persuade the other. In an entrepreneurial conversation, people learn about each other and discover common goals. As ways of working together become defined and developed, one entrepreneurial conversation can lead to another and often to many entrepreneurial conversations.

The Three Powerful Components of the Entrepreneurial Conversation

Engaging in entrepreneurial conversations will enable you to communicate effectively with anyone, be they colleagues, your kids, or the local bank loan officer. Once you have learned to engage in entrepreneurial conversations, you will be able to steer yourself toward success in any endeavor.

To harness the power of the entrepreneurial conversation you must adhere to three components:

- *Think* about other people's goals more than yours by researching their real issues (those topics of importance to them) while also being completely knowledgeable about your own concepts, abilities and attitude.
- *Listen* carefully and ask questions thoughtfully so you encourage the other person to listen, too; be yourself and find something to like in others so you can uncover mutually beneficial goals.
- *Speak* effectively about your ideas and be honest about your skills and commitment to long-term relationships; avoid small talk and elaborate presentations.

These three components of the entrepreneurial conversation are essential in every interaction you will have with other people, whether you are an entrepreneur seeking a bank loan, a parent talking to your child, or a manager discussing assignments with staff members. We return to these components throughout this book because they are so vital to the concept of building mutually beneficial, long-term relationships.

Take the obvious, add a cupful of brains, a generous pinch of imagination, a bucketful of courage and bring to a boil.

nard M. Baruch (1870–1965)
ancier and philanthropist, when asked for
recipe for success

Warning Signs that Your Conversation *Is Not* Entrepreneurial

When you *debate*, rather than *converse*, you bring the dialogue with the other person to a screeching halt. Warning signs that your conversation is not entrepreneurial include:

- Believing that your conversation is something you can win.
- Looking forward to the other person saying how right you are and how wrong he is.
- Becoming defensive.
- Becoming sarcastic.
- Allowing your prejudices to interfere with your judgment.
- Being bothered by minutiae, such as the other person's hairstyle.
- Noticing that you haven't asked a question that furthers honest inquiry for a long time.
- Thinking about what you want for dinner.

Signs that Your Conversation *Is* Entrepreneurial

When you have mastered the art of the entrepreneurial conversation, you will know that you are successful when one or more of the following happens:

- You keep thinking that the other person "gets it."
- You lose track of the time.
- You are overwhelmed by the exciting things you want to say.
- You feel optimistic.
- You can't decide which one of many options you should pursue.
- You want to work with the other person for a long time.

Because an entrepreneurial conversation is a way to work toward creative solutions in a non-adversarial way, people who think, listen and speak effectively are considered creative and easy to work with. Because the entrepreneurial conversation is a way to create possibilities and turn them into reality, people who think, listen and speak effectively are regarded as "doers" who accomplish their goals.

Wisdom
of the
Entrepreneurial
Masters
Robert Ezrapour

Robert Ezrapour was born and raised in Tehran while the Shah of Iran ruled from his opulent Peacock Throne. Shortly after Robert came to the United States to attend Lehigh University, the Shah was overthrown by the Ayatollah Khomeini, who instituted a reign of religious terror and oppression. Robert's family business was seized and his relatives were in grave danger. When he realized that it was impossible to return home, Robert decided to stay in America and smuggle his family out of Iran. One by one they arrived safely on American shores.

After Robert graduated and earned an MBA, he took a job with American Express. His fluency in Arabic, Farsi, French and English enabled him to become a valuable asset in their Middle Eastern markets.

Robert eventually realized that he was not cut out for corporate life. He yearned to launch his own entrepreneurial ventures and returned to America, where he joined the rest of his family in New York City. He and some partners built a successful electronics business and a textile company, but Robert felt these industries were unpredictable and subject to cutthroat competition, which he found unsavory. He decided to try the real estate business, although he had a lot to learn.

Robert looked at every deal he could find, whether it was a vacant lot, a strip mall, or an apartment house. "I knew next to nothing about real estate," Robert admits. "I needed to learn everything and learn it fast. Sellers and brokers were absolutely the best teachers."

So Robert Ezrapour acquired the first component of being a successful entrepreneur: He learned how to think like an entrepreneur and he became knowledgeable.

The enthusiasm Robert brought to every conversation and meeting also won people over. He is also blessed with a warm personality, a relaxed manner and a terrific sense of humor, qualities that make other people feel comfortable with him immediately. "Well, yes," he says modestly, "I do like to talk with people, but I think when I asked everyone so many questions because they knew more than I did, they felt good about themselves. They were the experts and they liked sharing information, so they liked me, too."

And Robert acquired the second component of being a successful entrepreneur: he learned how to listen like an entrepreneur and he was deemed likable.

Robert impressed people not only with his willingness to learn, but also with his forthrightness. He made sure he was on time for every appointment. "This was really important," he says, "because I usually met brokers at the real estate sites. If I was late, it would mess up the rest of the broker's day." As soon as Robert realized that a certain property wouldn't work for him, he was honest and spoke to the brokers and sellers immediately. "I wouldn't string them along and they knew I would work with them if they found the right deal for me." He also got down to business quickly, without engaging in small talk. "These were busy people," he says. "I respected the value of their time."

And Robert acquired the third component of being a successful entrepreneur: He learned how to speak like an entrepreneur and he became credible.

After considering many options, Robert purchased a small shopping center. His investors were pleased with their financial returns and were impressed by Robert's honesty and hard work.

After several years in business, Robert saw a tremendous opportunity to become a developer of low-income and middle-income housing. Property acquisition costs were reasonable, and government financing was available for some of the capital. Many developers shied away from governmental financing because the rules prevented the properties from being sold for at least thirty years. Robert saw this situation as a way to capitalize on his willingness to be a long-term player.

Robert's network of contacts in the real estate industry had expanded exponentially. His ability to think, listen and speak like a successful entrepreneur extended to his contractors, whom he paid handsomely and also invited to invest with him in the properties, giving them a strong incentive to do their best work. He joined with city agencies to identify potential development sites and he encouraged tenant and block associations to improve their neighborhoods. He gave his investors and bankers honest, detailed and accurate projections—and then made those projections come true. He stressed that his apartments were well designed and built, so he could attract tenants who would value living in one of Robert's buildings.

The people who joined forces with Robert trusted him to make the right decisions, and they relied on his credibility to deliver what he promised. Because of his openness and willingness to share in his success, Robert was well liked. His winning personality was an asset, but it was his ability to meet the expectations of his funders, partners, contractors and tenants that made working with Robert so satisfying.

Robert's company continues to flourish because he has created a strong network of people ready, willing and able to deliver the resources he needs to bring his ventures to fruition. He has learned how to think, listen and speak like a successful entrepreneur. "I treat everyone as if we are going to be working together forever," Robert says.

2 Think like a Successful entrepreneur

"Look before you leap" and "Think before you speak" are platitudes for a very good reason—they're true! You can still be an entrepreneurial person with ambitious goals and enthusiasm for your skills and concepts without being foolhardy. Thinking before speaking is absolutely essential for anyone who wants to engage in productive entrepreneurial conversations. It prepares you for questions, builds your confidence and helps create a setting for success.

We identify several aspects of thinking that will help you establish the most effective atmosphere for each entrepreneurial conversation. They are:

- **Be knowledgeable.** Do the research so you can learn as much as possible about the people you will be meeting. You must also understand every aspect of your own skills and concepts.
- **Identify the real issues.** You must find out which topics are of greatest importance to the other person. This will be based on your research and by listening attentively.
- **Possess the right attitude.** Your frame of mind will affect what you say, how you say it, and how you are regarded by the other person. Understand your attitudes so you can be open and honest at all times.
- **Realize that first impressions count.** You will have very little time in which to make a professional impact on the other person. Know how you come across to others and use the first few moments of your meeting to establish your personality and credibility.

Let's take a closer look at these aspects of thinking to see how they can help you engage in the most effective entrepreneurial conversations.

Be Knowledgeable

Think about a time in your life when you faced an important decision such as buying a house, choosing a medical treatment, or making a career move. Now remember who was trying to influence you at the time—a realtor, a doctor, or a potential employer. Wasn't that person's knowledge of the situation key to her influence over you? Perhaps you even said to yourself, "This person really seems to know what she's talking about. Maybe I should go with her recommendation."

We have a colleague who moved to a new city and went shopping for a house with a broker. In one afternoon the broker got lost three times, couldn't answer simple questions about neighborhood schools, and drove our friend to the same house twice. By the next day, he had found a new broker.

Within large organizations, power generally comes from the position a person holds, but a very close second is the power of knowledge. We know a woman we'll call Marie, who was the assistant to the president of a college. While college presidents came and went, Marie was always there. She knew the organization, the people, the rules and the history. This knowledge gave her tremendous power, and when she retired, the president's office became much less central to the life of the college.

There Is No Replacement for Knowledge, and Lots of It

If you're starting your own business, you must discern a potential investor's tolerance for risk. If you're a salesperson you must know whether your product or service is appropriate for potential clients. And if you're a boss, you must understand your employees' expectations about salaries and promotions.

In addition, you must know as much as possible about your product, service or profession. Make a list of all the possible questions another person might have about your skills. Think about the answers. Then have a trusted and knowledgeable friend, family member or colleague ask you difficult questions. If you can't answer them, get the answers. Once you're in an actual meeting it's better to say, "That's a great question, but I'll get back to you on that after I've thought it through more." Don't make a statement you can't support later.

Do Your Homework

There has never been a better time in history to obtain information.

Between the Internet and electronic resources available in virtually every library and organization, doing research is fast and easy. Before speaking with prospective clients, research their industry, products, competitors, needs and goals. Learn about potential investors by analyzing the ventures they have funded. Before meeting with your employees, read some of their internal memos or review their resumes.

If you're a physician, train your staff to find out the patient's basic symptoms when the appointment is scheduled and review the file right before you see the patient. We knew a man who had an operation to remove his gall bladder, and during his post-operative check-up, his physician asked how he was feeling since his hernia was repaired! This is not a good way to build confidence or to establish the right atmosphere for an entrepreneurial conversation.

Another important method of doing research is to schedule informational interviews with others in your field. As long as they are not direct competitors, they can be essential sources of information about issues you may not have considered, such as zoning or patent laws that might affect your concept. Most people will be flattered that you are seeking their expertise and will be happy to share their knowledge.

But remember to be honest about what you don't know or can't find out ahead of time. Once people are asked about their real issues (those subjects that are most important to them), they invariably open up and start talking—and you will learn even more by listening.

True Knowledge is knowing what you don't know.

Lewis Mumford (1895–1990)
Historian, city planner, philosopher

Know What You Don't Know

When celebrated historian and thinker Lewis Mumford uttered his famous statement, he was describing an important aspect of being truly smart. If you think you know everything, you won't bother listening to anyone else or learning anything new. Two people who both think they know everything can only debate, and debating is the antithesis of an entrepreneurial conversation.

Your task as an entrepreneurial person is to keep the conversation in balance, so you both know what you know, but also realize that you could learn a great deal more from each other. This keeps you open to listening and learning, contributing what you do know, and laying the groundwork for a relationship based on the benefits of your combined knowledge.

Many successful entrepreneurs we have worked with attribute their accomplishments to what they describe as "being a people person." They enjoy interacting with others and having the opportunity to meet a variety of people. But we have often wondered if one of the major ingredients in the success of these "people persons" was simply their ability to learn from others.

Identify the Real Issues

The entrepreneurial conversation should always be directed toward those subjects that are most important to the other person. We call these points of discussion the *real issues*. Because the real issues of an entrepreneurial conversation are the other person's issues, you must be not only knowledgeable, but also willing to learn more.

Uncovering the Real Issues

The real issues include measurable goals, such as projecting the return on an investor's stake, restoring a patient to good health, or establishing a salary cap for a new staff position. The real issues may also be subjective and harder to measure, such as when your new venture will become profitable, how curable the patient's disease might be, or how well a new employee will fit into your existing staff dynamics. The real issues are always substantive and they are always determined by the other person.

Focusing on the real issues moves the entrepreneurial conversation forward; any other subject stalls the conversation and reduces the chances of coming to an agreement to work together. Most people waste the opportunity to have an entrepreneurial conversation by not steering the discussion toward the other person's real issues. They think about their own needs instead.

For example, suppose you go into a shoe store to buy a pair of sneakers and the salesperson tells you, "We're trying to sell our stock of sneakers before the next season's models arrive, so we're offering 50 percent off on the second pair." That salesperson is telling you about the store's need to clear out its aging inventory. If, instead, the salesperson says, "If you find a perfect style and fit, this would be a great time to buy two pairs because we're offering 50 percent off the second pair," the salesperson has shifted the conversation to your needs and away from the store's needs. In the process, you are given a much more powerful reason to buy.

A banker will not be interested in how rapidly your business will grow. She cares more about your ability to pay back your loan on time. In fact, she may worry that if you focus on growth, you will pour so much money into early expansion that your poor cash flow will prevent you from meeting your loan payments, which is her primary real issue. A scientist applying for a research position will not be that interested in touring the spectacular new administrative wing you recently added to your building. In fact, he might worry that more funds are being funneled into girders and windows than will wend their way into his laboratory, which is his real issue.

The Real Issues Are about the Present and the Future

The real issues are always about the other participant's current and future goals. In his 1997 book, *How You Talk Is How You Lead*, Kim Krisco points out that many conversations that lead to constructive conclusions begin with descriptions of what has happened in the past, then move to a discussion of what could happen in the future, and end on the present to define tasks and actions.

If your conversations never move off talk of the past, then it is incumbent upon you to steer them into the realm of actions that can be taken in the present to create future possibilities. Over the years, hundreds of companies have hired Michael Corbett to help them develop advertising campaigns. Many of them had stopped advertising because they felt they had wasted money with no positive or clear impact on sales, but a conversation about the past wouldn't help them build their business in the future. When Michael shifted the discussion away from the past and onto future possibilities, the conversations led to productive results.

Possess the Right Attitude

Everything we do, say or see is determined by our own individual conscious or subconscious perspective. What's on your mind as you walk into a meeting has a tremendous impact on your ability to engage the other person in an entrepreneurial conversation. When you can think about the entire situation, including the attitudes you bring with you and your willingness to learn, you will begin to create a productive atmosphere for an entrepreneurial conversation. Once you focus on thinking about others and putting them first, you will be able to interact with them more effectively.

Let's imagine two salespeople. Salesperson A strides into a meeting with every client by thinking to himself, "I'm going in there to make myself a sale and earn a commission." Salesperson B says to herself, "I'm going to go in there and make myself a partner."

If the client says, "I'm interested in your product to help reduce my manufacturing costs," Salesperson A believes this is a buying signal and he tries to close the sale immediately by saying, "How about I write you up an order for a thousand of those to get you started?"

Salesperson B, however, doesn't view this as a closing opportunity. She sees it as a chance to begin an entrepreneurial conversation in which she can learn about the client's manufacturing process and how they can work together for the long term. Salesperson B will be more able to build a partnership and find the best and longest lasting application for her products.

The difference in approach comes from each salesperson's different attitude about goals.

We Don't See Things the Way They Are; We See Things the Way We Are

Think of the color red. If asked what a red light means, most of us would say, "Stop." But if you're a commercial airline pilot, a red light means you should steer clear of the 200-foot radio tower up ahead. It most definitely does not mean "Stop." If you're an accountant, red will conjure up dispiriting figures of losses and deficits, but if you're celebrating a red-letter day, you'll have candles to blow out or a diploma to frame. Being caught red-handed is an embarrassment, but a soldier is proud to be called red-blooded. A red-hot product will sell, but red tape will always bog you down.

The way we think about the color red depends on our training and our daily experiences, which make up our own separate points of view. Instead of seeing the color red in all its meanings, our focus may be too narrow and our response automatic. In short, we see the world not the way it is, but the way it appears to us.

Our individual points of view also involve how we interpret experiences from our personal frames of reference. If you see fishing as a way to make a living, your actions in a boat will be decidedly different from those of someone who sees fishing as recreation. A professional fisherman will search for the largest schools of fish, not the largest individual fish. He will drink coffee to stay sharp, not swig a six-pack of beer to relax.

You Can Change Your Point of View

The good news is that you can change your attitudes and limited points of view. You can learn what "red" indicates to others and expand your own restricted understanding of what "red" means to you. Open your eyes, survey the situation thoroughly, try to think like the other person, and adjust your perceptions accordingly. If your frame of reference limits your ability to establish effective relationships with others, you must learn to broaden your perspective.

We have known several doctors who had to manage their own major health problems at some point in their lives. All of them said that having the experience as a patient made them much better doctors. Why? Because they learned how to understand their patients' points of view.

Move beyond your usual automatic, easy response. Make a conscious effort to change your point of view and you will learn to understand the complete meaning of a particular job, a goal, a color, or a conversation. And you'll be thinking like a successful entrepreneur.

Realize that First Impressions Count

When your mother said, "You only get one chance to make a good impression," she was absolutely right. Research shows that within the first minute of meeting someone, people form an enduring opinion.

You might be the most organized person in the world, but if you're late to an appointment because of unforeseen traffic and then are forced to climb seven flights of stairs because the elevator is broken, you will walk into the other person's office sweaty and out of breath, creating a long-lasting impression of being disorganized.

On the other hand, if you arrive too early, and sit in the waiting room staring at the walls, you may look too impatient, or worse, as if you have nothing better to do with your time. If you're that early, wait in your car or go to a nearby coffee shop until it's closer to the time of your meeting.

In studying the interviewing process, University of Toledo psychologist Professor Frank Bernieri documented the extraordinarily rapid pace at which people form first impressions. Bernieri discovered that people who watched video clips of job applicants simply enter a room and shake hands with an interviewer reached virtually the same judgments about those people as the trained and experienced interviewer did after a 15-minute interview. You need to use that first sixty seconds to every advantage. Of course, you will have to be certain to maintain that good impression if a working relationship develops between you and the other person.

If you're the person being visited, the first impression you make is equally significant. Keeping people waiting is rude and makes them question your ability to handle their business, diagnose their symptoms or simply make them feel as if you value their time. An office with too few chairs and no coat hooks sends the message that you don't care about your visitors' comfort and may want them to leave as soon as possible. A messy desk implies that your guests' real issues might get lost in the shuffle.

Make a Positive Impact Immediately

To improve the first impression you make, be aware of it. Many people have no idea how they come across to others. They may feel they present themselves as aggressive or ambitious, but actually come across as soft-spoken and timid.

To help determine the first impression you're making, ask some people who will be candid to the point of pain to participate in an exercise with you. Schedule meetings either at their offices or homes and ask them to describe your manner, clothes, posture and speech within one minute of your arrival. If you're more likely to be visited by others, have someone do the same analysis after entering your office. An even more helpful demonstration is to videotape yourself in a similar businesslike practice session so you can actually watch yourself and draw your own conclusions about the impression you make.

Create a Setting for Success

The entrepreneurial conversation begins once you establish an atmosphere in which ideas can be exchanged freely. Being knowledgeable, adjusting your attitude toward open-mindedness, and making a good first impression will help build a solid foundation for an effective environment, but what you do next is critical.

Perhaps the best way to understand how to create a setting for success is to recall your own experiences with doctors. We knew a salesman who developed a persistent sinus infection. He obtained a referral to a physician who was reputed to be a top specialist. When he called the doctor's office to make an appointment, the salesman was put on hold, disconnected once, put on hold again, and generally treated rudely. As soon as he arrived at the physician's well-appointed office, he had to pay in advance, and then had to wait for an hour and a half before actually seeing the doctor in the examining room.

When the doctor finally examined his patient, he seemed rushed and annoyed to be burdened with such a mundane complaint. Twice he left the examination room to take care of other business. Once he took a call from his contractor to discuss a pressing matter about the construction of his swimming pool. He then tried to repeat a test he had forgotten he had already done. After he rendered his diagnosis, the salesman left to find another doctor.

No matter how qualified or capable this doctor might have been, the atmosphere he created was simply horrible. He and his staff failed to establish a welcoming, relaxing office environment and never placed the patient's needs or feelings first. The doctor never stayed focused long enough to engage in an entrepreneurial conversation that could have led to a rewarding, long-term doctor-client relationship.

At the other extreme, we recall an investment banker who told us about taking her mother to a doctor who established a superb setting for success. He saw them within ten minutes of the scheduled appointment time, and ushered them into his office where he had two chairs available in front of his desk. He focused on the older woman's complaints, asking thorough questions and listening patiently for her answers. The physician also showed no evidence of time pressures and demonstrated true concern for the woman's symptoms. At one point, the doctor reached over and simply held his prospective patient's hand. It was only then that the doctor took the elderly woman into the examining room. That first meeting began an enduring doctor-patient relationship that has lasted twenty-five years.

Your Place or Theirs

You have an obligation to create the right environment whenever you have an entrepreneurial conversation, whether you are the visitor or the person being visited. Possessing the right attitude and the willingness to uncover the other person's real issues can have a major impact on the other participant's response, whether you're in her office or yours. If you're exploring options on how to treat your bad back, you may distrust the doctor who talks only about surgery without discussing other options, such as physical therapy. Establishing the right atmosphere creates a strong sense of equal footing and an environment that is comfortable enough for everyone to exchange information and ideas openly.

If you are an investment banker or physician in your own office, you have almost total control over the setting for meetings with your staff or potential clients. Use this advantage to make others feel comfortable. Remember to shift your frame of reference so you are considering their issues and their goals before you discuss mutual solutions.

On several occasions we had the chance to observe a financier who is a master of establishing the best environment for an entrepreneurial conversation. He is a very unpretentious person whose office is a relaxed place with interesting photos and objects. He doesn't stay behind his desk for meetings, but sits with his other guests in an informal circle of chairs arranged around a coffee table.

His own manner, the physical setting, and the way he demonstrates that he has the time and interest to listen to his guests as equals, all contribute to establishing a context for a balanced and responsive discussion. The result is an entrepreneurial conversation that often produces a conclusion no one has anticipated, yet which still exceeds everyone's expectations.

There will be times, of course, when you will have little control over the circumstances of a conversation. If the meeting does not provide the atmosphere that is conducive to holding an entrepreneurial conversation, you may have to find another doctor or a more receptive loan officer. But by learning all you can about the situation in advance and concentrating on your own attitude, you will be able to foster an atmosphere of equality and openness, at least on your part.

Even in the noisiest surroundings, you can indicate that you will give your undivided attention to the conversation by visibly turning off your pager or cell phone at the start of the meeting. Adjusting your chair so you can make good eye contact with everyone in the room enables others to see you as they ask you questions—and listen to your answers.

When you cannot control the physical setting for your entrepreneurial conversations, meeting people in their offices will still provide other advantages, such as giving you a sense of their work environment and how they interact with their colleagues. If a relationship does not emerge from the meeting, you gave it your best shot and you put your knowledge to work—and learned something new.

Wisdom
of the
Entrepreneurial
Masters
Milt Kamen

During the five decades that **Milt Kamen** owned men's clothing manufacturing businesses and stores, he learned to think about his products and his customers and how to bring the two together. His understanding of what his customers wanted was as important as his vast knowledge of wool and weaves. He also had to make certain that both he and his sales staff at Gramercy Park Clothes possessed the right attitude about making sales.

When he dealt directly with customers buying suits, Milt learned what they were thinking by talking to them, asking questions, and, most importantly, listening carefully to their answers. He realized that they were busy people with many shopping options, so he created what he called "allure" by opening up his factory so people could buy directly from his manufacturing plant at a discount. "Customers felt it was like having an uncle in the business and being able to buy right from the manufacturer," Milt explains. "We had the sample fabrics there and tailors on hand to do the alterations." Milt's advertising supported this image by stressing lower prices and better service.

When Milt opened retail stores outside of his factory, he continued to create a setting for success. He watched his new customers carefully. He observed that they often responded to first impressions and were drawn to salespeople with whom they felt comfortable, so he employed people with a variety of personal styles and different backgrounds. By giving his customers a superior, relaxed, but attentive buying experience, Milt also made certain that they would return.

Another aspect of Milt's extensive knowledge about his products and customers was his understanding of the thorny issue known as "buyer's remorse." Almost anyone who has purchased a major item knows the wave of uncertainty that can occur afterward. Milt's strategy was to teach his sales staff to understand the complete process of buying a well-tailored suit made from excellent fabric.

"If the sale is handled properly, then buyer's remorse never becomes an issue," he says. "I made sure my salespeople were knowledgeable about the longevity of the fabric and the fact that we would re-tailor the suit at no cost if the customer needed alterations, even long after the suit was purchased. This showed that we believed in our product and believed that our customers' satisfaction was extremely important."

As a purchaser of fabrics and other clothing manufacturing items for more than twenty-two years, Milt also met with hundreds of salespeople in addition to thousands of customers.

He knew when he was being manipulated by a salesperson and when he was being honestly approached with the right attitude.

One of his best encounters was with a salesperson who, in a quiet and conversational tone, introduced himself, as Milt remembers it, along these lines: "My company wants to do business on a continuing basis with firms that profit most from what we do. Although I've done my homework about your needs the best I could from the outside, it would be helpful if you could tell me more." Milt says, "It was with this introduction that this salesperson began a conversation on how he could help us benefit from a relationship with his firm. In fact, that's just what happened. I knew he cared about my needs and he wasn't just thinking about a quick sale."

Milt says, "It's crucial for salespeople to be knowledgeable and credible. If they are, then customers are reassured about their decision to buy. Professional, effective business people," continues Milt, "are always communicating reassurance to their customers either implicitly or explicitly. They demonstrate that knowledge and the right attitude are everything."

3 Listen like a Successful entrepreneur

Most successful entrepreneurs are thoughtful and attentive listeners. By being great listeners, they allow the other person to feel comfortable about sharing information openly. This enables them to uncover the real issues of an entrepreneurial conversation quickly and respond to them productively.

Listening attentively is one of the most effective ways to show that you care about others, respect their opinions and that you are worthy of their time and attention.

Being a great listener just makes great business sense!

Listening is the single skill that makes the difference between a mediocre and a great company.

Lee A. Iacocca
(1924–)
businessman,
former president
Chrysler Corporati

Be a Great Listener

Listening is essential to holding an entrepreneurial conversation. Train yourself to ask the following question whenever you're talking: Would I be better off listening?

Becoming a great listener is not as easy as you might imagine. Many enthusiastic, ambitious people dash into conversations breathlessly without giving others time to think, react or speak. Most of us are also uncomfortable with silences that naturally occur during conversations, and we often rush in to fill the void without realizing that this is an opportunity for others to speak.

Disciplining yourself to focus on listening will dramatically improve the effectiveness of your entrepreneurial conversations. When other people see that you're listening to what they're saying, you're actually encouraging them to say more. This gives you an opportunity to learn about their real issues, which increases the likelihood of creating possibilities together.

A banker we know who is an expert listener often begins his meetings by mentioning a recent business issue in the news, asking his guests their opinions and then listening completely to their answers. He conveys that he has the time and interest to understand their thoughts not only on this subject, but on the main topic of the meeting as well. The resulting discussion makes people realize that they are being treated as equals, not supplicants begging for financing.

Being a poor listener can have a disastrous impact on relationships. We worked with a doctor who ran a major program at a large hospital. He opened his meetings by challenging and criticizing his staff to the point of questioning their honesty. If a staff member attempted to respond, the doctor became even more combative.

Over time, his staff learned to always agree with him, promising him anything he asked for (although he rarely got what was promised), and hoping he would leave them alone and move on to another target. He was simply the worst listener we ever encountered. His opportunities to learn how to be a good listener have diminished substantially now that his staff is quitting in droves.

Are You Really Listening?

We have seen more entrepreneurs talk their way out of making sales or attracting investors than talk their way into making sales or attracting investors. You will do more to build a relationship and establish the right atmosphere for an entrepreneurial conversation if you listen more than you talk.

In their book *Difficult Conversations: How to Discuss What Matters Most*, Douglas Stone, Bruce Patton and Sheila Heen explore some important aspects of successful listening. The authors' research, which grew out of their participation in the Harvard Negotiation Project, makes the following points about successful listening:

- **Listen authentically.** Feigned interest or listening to feedback only on selective points that further your own benefit actually shut down the other person's involvement. Avoid faking interest through body language, such as leaning forward in your chair.
- **Don't disguise statements as questions.** "Wouldn't you agree, Mrs. Quagmire, that the Supervac is the best vacuum cleaner you have ever seen?" is not really a question for the purpose of learning, but a rhetorical question for the purpose of manipulating a self-serving answer from the other person. This type of false question puts people off and does not further the conversation.
- **Don't be a television trial lawyer.** You're not questioning a witness. Stone, Patton and Heen caution against conversations that sound like legal cross-examinations. An example is the entrepreneur who says, "Didn't you say previously, Mrs. Quagmire, that you would invest in my Supervac if I demonstrated it on your office rug?" This type of question and the tone in which it is usually delivered casts you as an adversary, not as a person trying to establish a mutually beneficial working relationship.

- ***Don't restate points with surreptitious changes.*** One of the more annoying techniques is restating what the other person says, but with some barely perceptible alteration. The investor admits, "Yes, I'm familiar with your vacuum cleaner," and the entrepreneur says somewhat later in the conversation, "As you said, you're familiar with the excellent reputation of my Supervac." This is a manipulative and fundamentally dishonest technique and has no place in an entrepreneurial conversation.

Perhaps you've experienced some of the following scenarios:

- The potential employer who just keeps talking while ignoring your obvious desire to say something, including that you're ready to accept the job.
- The employer who discusses what he imagines your objections to the job might be, and in the process, plants those issues in your mind.
- The real estate broker who keeps telling you how much you'll like this two-story house, even though you asked her to show you only one-story houses.
- The colleague whose constant talking alienates you and ends any chance of holding an entrepreneurial conversation.

We accompanied an entrepreneur as he made a call on a prospective client. The potential customer ran a consulting company and had been looking for a system his staff could use when working off-site, but he was unable to find the specialized software application that would run on a portable, PC-type computer. He heard of the entrepreneur's company and arranged for a demonstration of his product.

The entrepreneur brought his portable computer, and in a few minutes had it running the software. In less than three minutes, the president of the company said, "This is exactly what I've been looking for." The entrepreneur, intent on showing how well prepared he was, ignored this statement and continued his presentation without letting anyone else speak. Instead of stopping for comments and questions, he went on to discuss features of the next version of the software and the smaller size and lighter weight of the upcoming generation of portable computers, which were due out in six months. After finishing his thorough demonstration, he asked the company president what he thought. The president said, "It's interesting, but come back and see me in six months."

Clarify Only What You Don't Understand

Many old-school techniques teach people to hear what the other person says and then restate the information back. "So, Mrs. Bottlenose, what I hear you saying is that you first opened your chandelier emporium in 1967 and have been selling chandeliers ever since. Is that correct?"

This kind of talk is unnatural in normal conversation and it's confrontational. It sounds like what it is: a pre-scripted monologue with nouns and names slipped into the text like a computerized letter.

Likewise, a question such as, "Does that mean, Mrs. Bottlenose, that you learned after six years in business that people who live in houses with eight-foot ceilings rarely buy four-foot long chandeliers?" might clarify a point, but prevents the other person from speaking freely and gives you negligible information.

Both participants certainly need to be clear about what is being said, so if you don't understand a point being made, ask for clarification. People engaging in entrepreneurial conversations focus on listening and interrupt only to ask questions when they truly don't understand a statement. The more you hear what the other person has to say, the more likely you are to gather the information you'll need to build a productive relationship. So try not to interrupt, except when the conversation is drifting away from the real issues.

Keep Your Ears Open

People often reveal their real issues when they're engaged in an entrepreneurial conversation. "I've always seen myself running a division here," an employee might say. A bank loan officer may mention that "We really want to invest in revitalizing our downtown rather than supporting another shoe store out in the mall." Goals that people are committed to are the goals they are most motivated to achieve—and talk about.

We know a man we'll call Dave, who owned a business that manufactured furniture for restaurants and offices. He was a wonderful boss, he made high-quality products, and he had a group of loyal customers. When Dave discussed his business, he enjoyed describing novel designs for one-of-a-kind pieces of furniture, many of which had limited commercial value in the restaurant and office trade, which focused on easily replicated designs.

Listening to Dave, we realized that he valued the artistic aspect of his work far more than the commercial aspect. We learned a few months later that after many years in business, Dave sold out to his partner so he could pursue individual projects commissioned by a small group of customers. "I was surprised by how much I had missed the design work," Dave said, "and how wonderful it was to begin all over again making singular, beautifully finished pieces of furniture."

Well, it wasn't a surprise to anyone who had listened to Dave talk about his restaurant furniture business. Pay attention to these revelations because they can become the basis for identifying the real issues. And once you identify the real issues, you can move the entrepreneurial conversation on to developing possibilities for meeting those needs and fulfilling those desires.

Silence May Be Golden, but What You Hear after a Silence Is Often a Pearl

Many people abhor silence in a conversation. They think that silence means the end of the meeting, or they experience it as some sort of negative vibe. In fact, it scares them and they rush in to fill the void by blurting out anything. But silence represents a great, and often ignored, opportunity because often what follows this silence is a statement of importance. Michael had a meeting with the owner of a retail food store to talk about the retailer's media plans. The retailer paused and rather than ask another question or say something else, Michael just let the pause continue. After what seemed like a long time, the retailer said, "You know, I have always had the dream of growing my business into a chain of stores." That was the pearl that—once stated—allowed Michael to work with him to accomplish his dreams.

Nonverbal Communication Isn't Everything It's Cracked Up To Be

When you're in a meeting and feel that someone likes you or doesn't like you, yet that person hasn't uttered a single word, you are experiencing the nonverbal communication of a conversation. Successfully interpreting these cues can help you overcome feelings of rejection and lead to more effective entrepreneurial conversations. But giving too much weight to these messages can lead you astray.

Nonverbal communication includes the interpretation of body language, an awareness of the other person's tone of voice, and the impact of first impressions, which is discussed more fully in *Chapter 2: Think Like a Successful Entrepreneur.* Misinterpreting these visual and aural cues can interfere with your ability to engage the other person in an entrepreneurial conversation.

Understanding these cues is essential in determining whether you or the other person are allowing prejudice to prevent an open exchange of ideas. Awareness of the cues is the first step to overcoming any negative influences on an entrepreneurial conversation, and becoming a far more effective listener.

Body Language: What It Is and What It Isn't

There are experts who have written extensive treatises about body language and what every gesture means. They insist that leaning forward during a meeting communicates interest, that yawning indicates boredom, or that crossed legs demonstrate impatience. But figuring out what all these motions and postures mean will distract you from the far more powerful elements of the entrepreneurial conversation. Constantly interpreting the other person's gestures may cause you to convey meaning through your own body language and you will waste time and energy on all that analysis instead of listening and speaking effectively.

Establishing a productive atmosphere for your conversation and making the real issues the focus of your meeting will express your interest and enthusiasm more than any superimposed body language. Leaning forward in your chair won't accomplish much if you're interrupting the other person to discuss your own needs. Listening, taking notes and asking attentive, thoughtful questions will indicate your interest far more effectively.

Watch Out for Misinterpreted Cues

During an entrepreneurial conversation you will learn a great deal that will be useful in the future, so don't let snap judgments interfere with your main task, which is to explore the possibility of working together.

If you're meeting with a room full of young MBA graduates, they may pepper you with challenging questions based on the subjects from their most recent final exams. Their tone of voice may seem disdainful because of their newly acquired credentials, but don't misinterpret the message you think they are sending. If they can offer the best support for your venture, you can learn to accept their behavior for what it is—youthful arrogance—and still forge a relationship that is mutually beneficial.

Edward once accompanied a relatively inexperienced salesperson on a call to a businessman who had bought ads on the salesperson's radio station in the past. The buyer was gruff to the point of being rude. He never left his chair and merely motioned Edward and the salesperson to seats in front of his desk. He asked what the salesperson wanted, and proceeded to play what was clearly an already in-progress game of solitaire on his computer. He never once looked up at his visitors. The salesperson introduced herself and her radio station, but looked at Edward as if to ask, "What should I do?" Edward signaled for her to continue, as if to say, "Ignore your interpretation of this guy's behavior. What do you have to lose?"

After a few moments, the salesperson asked, "Do you think advertising on our radio station can help your business?" The buyer, not pausing from his game of solitaire to even look up, asked, "What's special this week?" The salesperson answered haltingly that there was a sports sponsorship available and stated the terms. A long silence followed. When Edward determined that this silence had gone beyond an entrepreneurial pause, he nudged the salesperson, who then asked, "Did you hear what I said about the sports sponsorship?" The buyer, who continued to focus on his computer game, answered, "OK, I'll take it."

This buyer may have just been rude or indulging in some bizarre initiation rite for a new salesperson, but the salesperson has continued to do business with him and says, "He's gotten better, but not by much. At least I don't misinterpret his lack of attention as lack of interest in buying advertising time on our station."

Make Sure the Other Person Listens, too

You've probably listened to someone who is not really talking to you, but is just repeating a tired, old script. Like most people, you may have simply stopped paying attention. We often see this effect with advertising that uses clichés such as "new and improved," a phrase so worn out and discredited that people no longer pay any attention. To avoid shutting down the other people's interest and keep them listening, consider these suggestions:

- *Avoid generalities.* Statements such as "This will be good for you" mean nothing. Talk about the real issues that are relevant and specific to the other person's needs, based on what you have learned by doing your homework, by listening, and by engaging in an entrepreneurial conversation.
- *Avoid clichés.* Hackneyed statements such as "We're like a family here at Joe Blow Industries" are a mind-numbing turnoff. Avoid them like the plague.

- *Avoid grand promises.* Making big, bold claims such as how your telephone system, or legal representation, or catering service will magically transform someone else's business or bring an investor enormous returns are, at best, ignored. At worst, they crush your credibility.
- *Avoid judgments.* Harsh judgments can cloud your ability to understand the other person's real issues and are barriers to an entrepreneurial conversation. If you're selling telephone equipment and you state that the client's current system is ridiculously antiquated, you may offend the very person who selected the phones. If he decides to say something about this potentially embarrassing old system, he may choose to tell you that the system was purchased on an extremely limited budget and that he has finally convinced his boss to upgrade the equipment. This will save face for the client and prevent you from making a possibly insulting comment.

The Importance of Being Likable

Being liked has consumed business people for generations, maybe because so many negative associations about doing business have permeated our collective consciousness. *Caveat emptor* is the ancient Latin phrase for "buyer beware."

"Neither a borrower nor a lender be" is fatherly advice dispensed in Shakespeare's *Hamlet*, and P.T. Barnum, one of the most successful entrepreneurs ever, is purported to have uttered that infamous phrase, "There's a sucker born every minute."

It's no wonder we all worry about being taken for a ride when engaging in business conversations. We cannot trust people to like us for ourselves if we assume they are out to fleece us. And it's hard to like them if we feel we're being hoodwinked.

It's true that if you own the only gas station for a hundred miles, no matter how nasty you are, you'll still get customers. But in most business relationships, people have choices, so why give them a reason to look elsewhere?

People definitely prefer spending time with people they like. Since a great part of having a positive, mutually beneficial business relationship involves spending time conversing or working together, the person who is liked has, without a doubt, a great advantage over the person who is not. The good news is that there are effective ways of overcoming this concern about being liked—or liking others—so that you can engage in entrepreneurial conversations with almost anyone.

Be Yourself

By being who you are, you will be happier, more relaxed and, consequently, more likable. You simply can't be happy—or likable—by being someone you're not. You can't slip likability on as if it were an overcoat. You can't become a back-slapping, joke-telling, sports expert overnight just to get along with your clients, investors or employees if, in reality, you are a quiet, serious person who doesn't like sports and doesn't remember punch lines.

Choose a self and stand by it.

William James (1842-1910)
19th Century physician and philospher

Don't worry. The values you need to embrace in order to have entrepreneurial conversations with others have nothing to do with being anyone but yourself. We all have to start by accepting who we are, being true to that person, and liking that person. If you try to go through life with an "act," you will suffer the strain of maintaining it and, ultimately, your false front will be revealed. Being yourself makes you more comfortable and makes other people more comfortable being with you, which is really the best way to begin any conversation.

Once you trust being yourself, all of your thinking, listening and speaking will come more naturally. You'll soon realize that your research into other people's fields does not require a Ph.D. Doing your homework enables you to know what you don't know, so you're open to asking questions in order to learn more. Speaking persuasively does not mean you must learn to manipulate others, but it does demand that you be knowledgeable and enthusiastic about your product or service. And once you accept yourself, listening becomes a pleasure. You will no longer be talking to fill a void or out of nervousness that the other person doesn't like your idea—or you. You'll be secure enough to take a chance on hearing what the other person has to say. It is only through an honest, open dialogue that a true entrepreneurial conversation can emerge.

"Doing for others creates love for them."

—*John J.B. Morgan (1888-1945)*
author of How to Keep a Sound Mind

Look for Something to Like in Others

Finding something to like in other people is a great stimulant to having them like you. To be candid, liking others isn't always easy and sometimes simply won't happen. If the other person refers to his female colleagues as "girls," when you consider them to be women, you will have a hard time overcoming your negative reaction. But if you try, you can usually find something to admire in the other person—perhaps his hard work ethic, his belief in his company's product, or at the very least, his elegant tie.

As one consultant told us, "I had trouble liking the CEO who kept talking about basketball, a sport I've never followed, but I recognized that the enthusiasm and devotion he felt for his home team was similar to how he felt about his company. I read up on the team and actually watched a game," she said. "I still didn't like basketball, but I admired his passion and knowledge. He gave that same energy and commitment to supporting my consulting project. He became one of my biggest fans and recommended me to his colleagues, even though I still cringe a little when he starts talking about rebounds and field goals."

In the entrepreneurial conversation, the concept of likability depends on your attitude, not on using techniques that manipulate people into liking you. Your attitude toward yourself and the people you deal with, helps create a productive atmosphere for the entrepreneurial conversation.

Of course, the biggest boost to liking others is engaging in entrepreneurial conversations with them. When you realize you have helped your client buy something truly useful, or your student learn something truly important, you will realize the truth of Professor John Morgan's statement that doing for others creates love for them. Well, "love" is a pretty strong word. We'll settle for "like."

Here are some key concepts to keep in mind as you uncover a more likable you:

- Remember that your task is to do something for the benefit of the person you are speaking to, as well as for yourself.
- Remember to be open to new ideas so you reassure other people that you are easy to work with and interested in their needs.
- Remember to be yourself. All types of people from varying backgrounds and with different personalities are successful.
- Remember to learn from everyone you meet. The adage, "Everyone is enlightened, but me," suggests that you should always be listening to others and learning from them.

- Remember to find a little something to like in everyone. It's easier to be liked if you like others.

Don't Be Prejudiced

Research shows that preconceived ideas interfere with our ability to listen to and accept new information. People who are biased almost never see or hear the evidence to counter their prejudices. Many parents, for example, have a hard time recognizing the shortcomings of their own children. Individuals who are racist or sexist can't get beyond their prejudices, which encourages them to disregard entire groups of people.

As we discussed in *Chapter 2: Think Like a Successful Entrepreneur*, the tendency to see and hear what confirms our preconceived ideas can actually block our ability to think knowledgeably, truly listen to what someone else is saying and to speak openly.

Consider how you might behave if you're told that the person you're about to meet had a very favorable opinion of you. You would probably be warm, open and gracious, and you would likely elicit a similar response from the other person. If, on the other hand, you were told that the person had an unfavorable opinion of you, you would be more likely to be distant and cautious, and would be treated in kind.

We know an executive who manages sales and distribution for a pharmaceutical company. He complained that the doctors he called on treated him with disdain and never let him finish his sales pitch. He interpreted this as an indication of how highly educated professionals looked down on lowly salespeople. This prejudice made it difficult for him to engage his clients in entrepreneurial conversations and to form productive business partnerships for his company.

With our encouragement, the executive discussed his judgments openly and began to understand that his clients actually didn't have a great deal of time and that everyday work pressures prevented them from relaxing and conversing easily. Once he understood that his clients were acting rushed and distracted not because of him, but because of the nature of their jobs, the executive was able to let go of his prejudices and work more effectively with his harried clients.

He scouted the hospitals in advance to find reasonably quiet rooms where he could take his clients for brief meetings. Although the executive understood that physicians couldn't ignore their pagers, he always turned off his own cell phone and pager in front of them to indicate his commitment to the conversation. He also gave his clients the chance to tell him what they needed, instead of overwhelming them with his sales pitch. He became a better listener.

When his customers realized that he was making a sincere effort to be calm and attentive even in their hectic surroundings, they responded better. Since then, the executive's orders have increased dramatically.

By being aware of your judgments and working to create an environment that addresses and dispels them, you will be able to manage your opinions and engage others in effective entrepreneurial conversations. You will also become a far more masterful thinker, listener and speaker.

Don't Sit in Judgment

Both negative and positive judgments will shut down the creative brainstorming process that is central to an entrepreneurial conversation. When you criticize others' ideas, you build up their defenses and they stop participating. On the other hand, positive judgments stated too early in the conversation reinforce the belief that you have uncovered the right answer and you may suspend the process of inquiry into other, even better ideas.

In their book *Dialogue: Rediscover the Transforming Power of Conversation*, authors Ellinor and Gerard point out that the act of judging what someone else says—whether positively or negatively—interferes with one's ability to have a dialogue. To avoid the problems caused by judging, the authors urge people to suspend judgment so they can encourage others to bring up new ideas and allow these ideas to be fairly evaluated.

We believe that it is very hard to suspend judgments and suggest a more sensible approach. Be aware of the judgments you are making and then consciously look for evidence to the contrary. You will almost always find reasons for changing your judgments if you are honest and open-minded about your search. By bringing your judgments into the open and becoming conscious of them, you'll be able to free yourself from their constraints and become a more effective thinker, listener and speaker.

The most extreme example of the destructive power of positive judgments is what psychologist Irving Janis calls "groupthink" to describe what happens when people avoid independent judgment because they value group membership so highly.

We once worked with a company whose management had set ridiculously high sales goals. When we looked into the source of these goals, we found that the management team had only recently purchased the company. To make the inflated price they paid for the business seem reasonable, they had to achieve incredibly ambitious sales growth. When we discussed these clearly unattainable goals with management, they were united and adamant in their defense of their joint decision. Nothing could break the cycle of "groupthink" that made them all believe in the positive judgment that they could achieve these goals—except time.

Wisdom
of the
Entrepreneurial
Masters
Xiaoning Wang

When **Xiaoning Wang** began taking her son to neighborhood playgrounds near her home in Brooklyn, New York, she noticed a number of Caucasian parents pushing Chinese babies in strollers. Smiling at the babies pulled Xiaoning into conversations with the parents, who, when they learned that she was from China, barraged her with questions. "They'd ask me where they could sign up for Chinese language lessons or buy Chinese books and music tapes for their kids," she says. "They wanted to keep their babies in touch with their Chinese heritage, but they didn't know how." Although Xiaoning couldn't answer their questions, her curiosity and her entrepreneurial spirit were piqued.

Xiaoning was aware of China's firm "one child per family" policy, but she never knew that it had generated so many foreign adoptions. "Listening to these parents who yearned for a connection to China convinced me that a business providing them with Chinese products could be possible," she says.

Xiaoning logged on to the Internet to learn more about families with adopted Chinese babies. She soon discovered that these parents were not only Internet savvy, but were also blessed with good educations and comfortable incomes. "I was even more convinced that my business could work," she says, "and I knew the right medium to reach my customers—the Internet."

On her next trip to China, Xiaoning sourced the products her potential customers wanted. She knew she could purchase, market and ship her items and still charge reasonable U.S. prices. When Xiaoning returned to Brooklyn, she showed her samples to the adoptive families in her neighborhood. "They bought everything," she says, "so I took some money from my savings account and set up my Web site." The name for her business came to her quickly. "I wanted to express that these babies had sprouted in China but were growing here," she explains. ChinaSprout.com was born.

Xiaoning immediately began hearing from customers around the world. "They told me about other items they wanted," she says, "so we implemented a home page feature to make product recommendations easy." Xiaoning soon added a bulletin board discussion group so her customers could share information. "I wanted them to be in touch with each other like those families in my neighborhood playground," she says, "so I tried to create a sense of community. It worked."

Because Xiaoning spent so much time listening to her customers, she was able to grow her company in unexpected ways. "One of my early customers told me about associations designed to help parents of adopted Chinese babies," she explains. "I joined these groups and now I can send ChinaSprout.com promotions to over 13,000 families on their lists."

About a year after her Web site was launched, Xiaoning's customers told her that they wanted their relatives to know about ChinaSprout.com. "I hadn't really thought about these extended family members and friends," she explains, "but by listening to my customers and setting up a place on the site for them to add additional names and addresses to my lists, I increased my customer base by 200,000. I think this is a good example of how I include my customers in every single contact and how I really listen, listen and listen to them all the time."

Within six months, ChinaSprout.com had turned a profit without Xiaoning ever having to reach beyond her personal savings account for start-up financing. In the first two years of business, ChinaSprout.com never experienced a month with less than triple-digit growth. From its initial catalog of less than a hundred products, the website now sells over 2,500 different items.

Xiaoning's commitment to engaging her customers in entrepreneurial conversations has grown along with her company. She manages to talk to as many as forty customers a day either by phone or e-mail. By listening to them, Xiaoning has discovered new markets for her products. She is currently reaching out to a network of American public schools that offer Chinese language and history courses. "They need educational materials that work in U.S. classrooms, and we know how to get the best," she says.

"Listening to those first parents in the playground gave me the idea for ChinaSprout. com," says Xiaoning. "And listening to my customers now is helping me grow my business. Thanks to my customers, I've been able to balance what I call the three Cs of business—commerce, content and community—to build a strong connection to our market. Listening to my customers lets them participate fully in my business and is the key to my success."

4 Speak like a Successful entrepreneur

Now that you've learned the importance of thinking and listening, you must master the art of speaking. When you speak you begin to establish your credibility with the other person by demonstrating your knowledge and your willingness to learn more.

Speaking clearly and eloquently in an entrepreneurial conversation enables you to identify topics for discussion (the real issues), propose solutions, make agreements, and implement plans. But don't worry too much about being eloquent. If you are knowledgeable and enthusiastic, this will almost always translate into eloquence.

Speak Face-to-Face

We all appreciate the convenience of the telephone, voice-mail and e-mail, but when you have a key decision to make, a relationship to form, or a deal to forge, nothing has yet replaced face-to-face contact. An in-person meeting shows a commitment of effort because it requires bridging any physical distance and it takes more time than other means of communication.

Face-to-face meetings are less subject to interruption and distraction. While talking on the phone, many people look through items on their desks or computer screens. If you're talking to someone on his cell phone, he may be driving a car, picking up his dry cleaning, or meeting his kids at school. You will rarely have a person's full attention when speaking to him on his cell phone.

E-mail and voice-mail are convenient for handling the quick details of everyday interactions, but they are rarely effective for building long-term relationships. Busy people often have an overwhelming number of e-mail and voice-mail messages and review them quickly to perform triage by ranking their importance. The delay between the arrival of messages and the response time can also create disjointed communication. This is scarcely the atmosphere in which to develop a relationship, brainstorm possible ways of working together, or come to a long-term agreement.

Finally, face-to-face meetings are best because they are the most fertile form of contact, imparting more information to each participant than any other means of communication. Meeting people in person allows you to see and hear them. You can understand their inflections, their pauses, their tones of voice and body language. If you're meeting someone in her own office, this will give you a sense of how she maintains her work space—is it messy or neat?—and how she interacts with her colleagues—is she friendly or domineering?

We do not believe in relying on interpreting body language to the exclusion of the content of what the other person is saying, but an in-person meeting still allows you to see how a person reacts nonverbally to ideas and statements. You will be better able to determine what is on the other person's mind without having to be a mind reader.

Question the Assumptions

When you engage in an entrepreneurial conversation, you will not only uncover the other person's real issues, but some of her underlying assumptions as well. Unearthing these underlying assumptions is often an archeological task, as most are not directly stated.

Clients may, upon hearing an idea, reject it because "that's not how our customers think." This statement invites exploration into how clients believe customers *do* think. A potential investor may say, "We've already invested in a pet store in that neighborhood," which means you should discuss the nature of that particular pet store, or how the investors define the parameters of the neighborhood. Maybe the other pet store deals only with exotic animals, such as snakes and lizards, and you will be selling fuzzy puppies and kittens that may make your plan far more attractive.

Charles F. Kettering (1876–1958) Inventor of the automobile engine starter and founder of Delco Electronics

When you question the assumptions, your entrepreneurial conversations will lead to ways to raise hypotheses and test them. For example, in meeting with representatives from a client bank, an ad agency can suggest various ideas: How would promoting mortgage loans work during various seasons? Has the bank considered extended hours before Christmas? Should new automated-teller locations be promoted by randomly giving customers at these machines an extra $20 when they get cash?

These kinds of questions educate the participants while raising and evaluating various assumptions. When an idea is finally worked up into a specific proposal, it has already been agreed to conceptually during the previous entrepreneurial conversations. Going into a meeting to pitch an idea is not part of an entrepreneurial conversation. Going into a meeting to uncover the other person's real issues and discuss the underlying assumptions will engage all the participants in effective, productive entrepreneurial conversations.

Chris Argyris, a professor at Harvard University who has researched organizational communication, presents a model of organizational learning in which the underlying beliefs, values and assumptions lead to desires, strategies and actions, which in turn produce results. After the results are in, some people loop back to reevaluate the desires, strategies and actions. Argyris calls this process single-loop learning. Others loop back to the underlying beliefs, values and assumptions that lead to the desires, strategies and actions, in a technique Argyris calls double-loop learning.

For example, two employees are applying for the same job opening in their company. One wants the promotion because she plans to leave the company and knows that moving from the higher position will be more beneficial. The other has applied because he's committed to a career in the company. Both employees have the same desires and strategies, but their motivations are based on very different underlying assumptions and values.

An entrepreneurial conversation should not stop at single-loop learning, but should include double-loop learning because, as Argyris's research has shown, organizations that practice double-loop learning are more effective at achieving their goals. Uncovering the underlying assumptions leads to breakthroughs in identifying the real issues, which furthers the process of the entrepreneurial conversation and creates more productive relationships.

Speak the Truth

Entrepreneurial conversations rest on a foundation of trust. Unless what you say is perceived as truthful, it will rarely elicit an honest response. A conversation is somewhat like a friendly game of catch, with ideas bouncing back and forth like a ball. But if the ball is a rotten tomato or a live hand grenade, a friendly exchange is impossible. If the ideas you proffer in a meeting are lies, manipulations or misstatements, an entrepreneurial conversation will be equally impossible.

Honesty in the first chapter in the Book of Wisdom.

Thomas Jefferson (1743-1826)
founding father, president

Honesty Is Still *the Best Policy*

Speaking the truth means that you can be relied upon to deliver what you promise, big or small. Promising to have the wedding cake at the reception before the guests arrive is clearly a major way that a baker's customers depend on him. Promising to send a copy of a pertinent newspaper article to a colleague, or answering an employee's questions honestly—no matter how insignificant—are all part of building credibility. Promises are meaningless without follow-through. People without credibility are usually ignored. Listeners become inattentive and unwilling to discuss the real issues. They often bring the conversation to a rapid and unfruitful conclusion.

Credibility is also amazingly fragile. Showing up on time is a simple but meaningful way to establish credibility and trust. Being late for a meeting communicates that you do not value the relationship or the other person's time, and it reflects negatively on your ability to accomplish what you promise.

Even in a long-established relationship, only one unfortunate incident can destroy credibility. We witnessed a tragic interaction between the presidents of two companies who had done business together for more than ten years. One company was a distributor of products and the other was a manufacturer with extensive product lines. When the president of the manufacturing company told the head of the distributor that they planned to add a new line, he asked the distributor to handle it along with their other products. The distributor said yes.

A few months later, when the president of the manufacturing company called to say that they were ready to begin distribution, the distributor said that he had a conflict of interest with the new product line from another client and would have to decline distribution. Feeling that the credibility of the distributor was damaged, the manufacturer moved all of his distribution to a competitor's firm.

Being credible means that you think clearly before you speak, that you double-check all the issues before you commit to a project, and that you promise only what you can deliver. Once you've established credibility, don't get lazy and let your reliability slip. Maintaining credibility is as important as establishing credibility.

Credibility is also based on ethics, including moral and legal issues. For us, the test for ethical behavior is simple: Are you focused on the long term and are you building a mutually beneficial relationship for you and the other person? Scam artists, crooks and perpetrators of corporate fraud all have one thing in common: They are looking to get away with something today without regard for the long-term consequences or the harm they cause others. If you focus on the long term and the effect your actions have on others, you will be working to build mutually beneficial relationships and you will be behaving ethically.

The Danger of Small Talk

Beyond a brief ice-breaker, an entrepreneurial conversation should not include topics such as the weather or sports. Brief discussions about your credentials are necessary to demonstrate that you are knowledgeable and credible, but small talk keeps the conversation going in circles when it should always move forward. And small talk will never uncover the other person's real issues.

Homework is absolutely essential to providing a foundation for a mutually beneficial dialogue, but no amount of research will fill in all the relevant information that can be determined during an entrepreneurial conversation. You need to understand the other person's ambitions, concerns and goals in order to engage in a knowledgeable give-and-take between equals—which is the essence of an entrepreneurial conversation. Small talk won't lead you there.

Here are some of the common signs that you're engaging in small talk:

- You have not yet uncovered the other person's real issues.
- You are caught in a cycle of saying things you have already said.
- You feel like a convenient prop for the other person's personal stories or political positions.
- You can't imagine how this conversation will lead to anything productive.

When you avoid small talk and discuss the real issues, you will notice that goals, opportunities and options are revealed in the natural flow of the entrepreneurial conversation. It is only through a dialogue of the real issues that you will be able to arrive at a mutually beneficial course of action.

The Entrepreneurial Presentation

Successful entrepreneurs who have developed a plan for working together with others by engaging in entrepreneurial conversations do not generally rely on presentations, which by their nature can be stilted, rigid, and not very conversational. However, a potential client or investor may expect some sort of low key presentation during the first meeting and may later ask for a proposal that sums up the agreed upon plan to work together. For example, if you are ill you can imagine having your doctor meet with you to review the test results and treatment options. Similarly, if you manage an organization and you have been planning to upgrade your computer system, you can have someone in your organization make a presentation summarizing what has been learned and the various decisions that now need to be made.

We'd like to offer some guidance on making entrepreneurial presentations:

- Don't use a rigid script. Be adaptable and allow for interaction.

- Stress the other person's real issues.
- Think in terms of offering recommendations, rather than just a presentation.
- Give credit for others' ideas.
- Allow time for questions and comments.

Indicate how your suggestions are the result of your previous entrepreneurial conversations and a refinement on the proposed working relationship that has already been discussed. By the time you are ready to make a recommendation, you have accomplished the following:

- You have completed extensive research on the other person's needs.
- You have been holding entrepreneurial conversations with at least one person in authority.
- You have created an in-depth list of possibilities together, ranked them and chosen the most appealing one.

Since the resulting recommendation is drawn from your entrepreneurial conversations, it is not just your suggestion, but a well-reasoned, mutual conclusion based on the other person's real issues. Sometimes a recommendation needs to be adjusted if new issues come to light, but it will generally be accepted most of the time if it results from a series of entrepreneurial conversations.

Use PowerPoint® — Don't Let PowerPoint® Use You.

When you make a presentation either at the beginning of your series of entrepreneurial conversations or after several meetings, you may need to use visual aids to explain some of the concepts that you have developed. Many people think that the proverbial "dog and pony" show requires a high level of production values to make a presentation appear professional and credible. If your audience believes that PowerPoint® or other visual aids indicate a high level of preparation, using these tools is a must.

Slides, overhead projectors and PowerPoint® presentations can also provide you with structure and help keep you focused. But for the person steeped in the art of the entrepreneurial conversation, there are important guidelines in using these tools:

- ***Be flexible.*** The slide show or PowerPoint® script is fixed ahead of time, but your presentation shouldn't be. Strive for an entrepreneurial spirit by being ready to deal with the issues audience members raise and the reactions they have. Your presentation will be greatly improved if you are able to skip slides, go over some material quickly and arrange topics in the order your audience expects to hear them, even at the last minute.

- *Strive to keep your presentation interactive.* Most people don't pay attention to presentations that aren't interactive. Turn off the lights, turn on the projector, introduce a speaker, and most people will tune out or even nod off. An entrepreneurial presentation can occur only if your audience is actively involved, not passively watching a performance.
- *Encourage people to ask questions or give comments.* Using presentation tools often discourages people from talking because they know that you're basically following a script, which can stifle one of the greatest assets of the entrepreneurial conversation: the ability to engage in a mutually productive discussion. Tell your audience in advance that you will take comments and questions at appropriate times during your presentation or at the end.

Keep any exposition of your ideas simple and flexible. Make changes to your PowerPoint® program or put revisions on a blackboard or easel to integrate new ideas into your presentation. By involving your audience and listening to their comments, you can make your presentation into an effective, adaptable entrepreneurial conversation.

It's OK to Say No

Remember that you are trying to have a conversation that builds a relationship of trust. If you realize during your entrepreneurial conversation that a potential relationship will be short term or unproductive for either participant, then feel free to say no.

When Do You End a Dead-end Relationship?

The sooner, the better! Some entrepreneurs believe that once they have gotten in the door to see potential clients or investors, they must continue to work forever to try to turn them into actual customers or funding sources. We know accountants, lawyers and investment bankers who have regularly lunched with potential clients for years without any reasonable expectation of forming a business relationship. And we have witnessed entrepreneurs who continue to pursue unlikely investors whose funding guidelines don't fit.

We look at it this way: When does a reasonable person stop trying to push a size-12 foot into a size-7 shoe? As soon as possible! This should be your guiding principle when you see that there is no application for your product or service to the other person.

This is not to say that nothing of value can come from these interactions. By being candid and saying to the other person, "Now that I have a better understanding of your needs, I can see that we won't be able to forge a mutually beneficial relationship," you will build a huge amount of credibility.

A potential client may develop a need for your product in the future, or an investment company may change its guidelines and want to fund a business like yours. If they recall your honesty about your product or service, they may decide to contact you. And if they respect your candor and enthusiasm, they may refer you to someone who is more likely to become an actual customer or investor.

The reverse is also true. If you know of another person or company that can provide the right service for a client, go ahead and make the referral. The other companies will be grateful for the contacts, and your reputation for cooperation and honesty will be strengthened immeasurably.

We know a New York City hardware store we'll call Acme, in a neighborhood with four other nearby hardware stores. Acme has a policy of telling its customers which of its competitors carry items that Acme itself doesn't have. This is a great service and has earned Acme a strong following because customers know that it is always the best place to try first.

Here are some examples of reasonable expectations for any potential relationship:

- That the other person not waste your time by keeping you waiting, canceling meetings at the last moment, or talking endlessly about irrelevant issues.
- That the other person be honest with you about his needs, such as delivery, price, product features or service. If you later find out that the other person was being demanding for the fun of it or misrepresented his authority to make decisions, then end the relationship or find another person within the organization to engage in entrepreneurial conversations.
- That your proposal for working together be answered by a certain time. Being endlessly strung out by someone who promises you an answer in the unspecified future is a waste of time and emotionally exhausting. It's reasonable for you to say that unless you receive an answer by a certain date, you can't work together.

Thinking and listening like a successful entrepreneur will enable you to uncover the other person's real issues and help you formulate an agreement to work together. Speaking eloquently about your skills will also establish your honesty, credibility and enthusiasm for your abilities and your desire to help others achieve their goals.

Wisdom
of the
Entrepreneurial
Masters
Don Wilson

Don Wilson is the founder and president of Optics for Research Inc., a technology company in New Jersey that manufactures and distributes high-quality components to the optics and laser industries. Don was always open to the idea of having his own business because he had seen his father, in his own words, "get shoved around and treated like meat" as the employee of a big company. In spite of this awareness, Don began his own career after earning his engineering degree by working for a large firm. But he soon felt frustrated. "I was spending more time watching my back," he says, "and wasting time on organizational politics than on competing in the marketplace." Don began thinking about alternatives and decided to go out on his own.

He set himself up as a manufacturer of optical components, such as filters and prisms, which he understood well and could help design. Don's experience and educational background equipped him with the knowledge to think, listen and speak as an equal with his customers about their work, their needs, and their concepts for new products. "Most of my best ideas came out of conversations with my customers," he says. Shortly after starting this first venture, Don was talking to a client who said he wished there were a catalog that carried the products he needed. Don immediately questioned the assumption that selling optical components didn't require catalogs.

"I'm good at categories," Don thought to himself. "Making a catalog should be easy for me." Don realized that the same organizational skills that made him an excellent engineer and salesperson also enabled him to classify the thousands of optical components used by scientists. He also learned that by having an open, entrepreneurial conversation with his customer, he had uncovered a mutually beneficial venture.

Don produced his first catalog. Some products he featured were from his own manufacturing plant, but if he believed that another company provided a better item, he included it in the catalog as well. He knew that his customers valued quality above all else in the products they bought and that is what he gave them. And they appreciated Don's honesty in admiring and promoting good products, even if they weren't his own.

Don's business was growing steadily in the early 1960s when the invention of the laser revolutionized the industry. Lasers, which utilize optical equipment, spawned many new applications for the components Don manufactured. Because Don's knowledge of his customers' needs was so highly developed, his company was perfectly positioned to beat the competition by moving quickly and by serving his customers well.

A few years after starting his business, Don noticed that instead of calling on his customers, his customers were calling on him. He had written a well-received scientific paper that many of his clients had read, and his reputation continued to spread throughout the optics industry. At a recent trade show, with hundreds of manufacturers displaying their wares in large booths surrounded by salespeople snagging passersby, Don and one of his employees sat in a corner as customers streamed up to them and described the products they needed.

One of Don's most successful products was developed from a customer's request. In the early 1980s, Don received a call from a client at Bell Labs in New Jersey asking if Don's company could make a product that kept laser-generated light moving in one direction. They discussed the idea and its specifications, and Don's team built a prototype. The resulting optic isolator quickly became essential to many new laser applications, and Don's company was again perfectly positioned to be the first with the best.

Don Wilson's career indicates that power comes from thinking about and understanding the customers' needs and placing them first. He has also thrived because he always listens to their suggestions and speaks to them as equals.

To this day, Don claims that he doesn't make sales calls and he doesn't consider himself a salesperson—but he does make lots of sales. This is because he holds entrepreneurial conversations with his customers that are based on his deep knowledge and understanding of their real issues. He shares his clients' interests in science and excellence; he understands their needs and fulfills them with superior products and service. "Basically, my clients and I have the same scientific interests and I'm a good listener," is how Don sums up his success.

5 the entrepreneurial Manager

Managers can use entrepreneurial conversations not only to be more effective bosses, but to create entrepreneurial organizations. While successful entrepreneurs use their conversational skills primarily with their external community, such as customers and investors, they can produce equally effective results with their internal community of employees and colleagues. The same is true for managers who oversee divisions within large organizations.

When managers engage in entrepreneurial conversations with their staff members, their employees are more likely to create innovative solutions to old problems and revitalize their enthusiasm for their work. Entrepreneurial conversations reinforce employees' best qualities, such as being knowledgeable and maintaining positive attitudes, enthusiasm, commitment, and the determination to do their best.

To become a successful entrepreneurial manager, you must use the entrepreneurial conversation in everyday interactions with staff and colleagues, from interviewing potential employees to communicating effectively during weekly staff meetings.

We will never forget witnessing the chairman of a company at a staff meeting following a record year that had exceeded all sales and profit goals. Instead of the thanks and kudos they were expecting, his staff was subjected to a forty-five minute diatribe about how bad the situation was. The chairman attacked the goals for the year, which he saw as ridiculously low. Then he launched into stories of other companies that had done better than his, even though they were in different industries and located in other countries. He ended by stating that he was being victimized by a lazy, self-interested and unprofessional staff. The lunch that followed was a quiet, sullen affair. It looked as if half of the employees were afraid they were being fed poison and the other half wished they were.

While an absolutely true story, this is not an extreme example. The outdated, old-school principles embodied by this company chairman are used in varying degrees by thousands of managers every day: threats, insults and negative comments are liberally administered to the staff. No achievement is good enough. No one should feel secure in her job. No one is encouraged to participate in an open exchange of opinions and ideas. For many managers, this attitude reflects how they are treated by their own bosses. For others, it is their best effort to spur better results.

But negative reinforcement absolutely doesn't work. By utilizing the positive reinforcement that is inherent in the entrepreneurial conversation, managers can unleash the unlimited power of a rededicated, reinvigorated staff.

A life is not important except for the impact it has on other lives.

Jackie Robinson (1919–1972)
First African American to play
Major League Baseball

Adhere to the Three Powerful Components of the Entrepreneurial Conversation

The strongest motivation for both managers and their staffs comes from a dedication to thinking, listening and speaking effectively at all times.

Let's review each of the components of the successful entrepreneurial conversation and see how they apply specifically to managers.

Think—Be Knowledgeable

You don't have to be able to perform every job under your direct management, but you do need to know what each job entails. Understanding every aspect of your company's business and every employee's responsibilities will provide a solid foundation for interactions with your staff. If an employee believes that you don't understand his duties, or that you have burdened him with too many extra tasks, ask him to write a memo about his real issues so you can respond with complete knowledge, not just your impressions of his frustration. Once he knows you grasp his real issues, you have established an open attitude and created a setting for a successful meeting.

Listen—Be Likable

Listening is the key to hearing the other person's real issues, connecting with her through shared experiences, and establishing the communication that is the hallmark of every entrepreneurial conversation. Being likable doesn't mean you must form fast friendships with your employees, but it does mean that you respect their talents and acknowledge their work in significant ways. It means that you are understanding and compassionate if they have temporary personal problems that might interfere with their productivity. It means that you will work together to find solutions to the challenges of being a manager with employees. And it means that you accept yourself by not trying to be someone you're not. And remember, always look for something in the other person to like.

Speak—Be Credible

Honesty is still the best policy in dealing with employees, too. You don't have to share trade secrets or discuss corporate policy changes before they happen, but you do have to tell employees how any shift in company management or goals affects their jobs. Don't entice your staff with carrots if you won't give the rewards when employees earn them. Don't promise the moon if you don't hold any power over celestial bodies. And don't make the mistake of praising where no praise is due. This will undermine the respect of the employee who isn't doing well and will cause other staff members to mistrust your judgment. Loss of credibility is a terrible fate. Avoid it at all costs. Remember that you are willing to question the underlying assumptions of a situation whenever you engage in an entrepreneurial conversation. In this atmosphere, your employees may even be able to suggest some solutions you might not have considered.

The Entrepreneurial Conversation Is a Power Tool for Management

The powerful principles of the entrepreneurial conversation work as effectively for managers as they do for entrepreneurs. Even when inheriting a dispirited staff that has been subjected to all the wrong motivators by a previous boss, entrepreneurial managers can establish a new and healthy relationship with their employees. The entrepreneurial conversation works internally as well as externally because:

- The entrepreneurial conversation is the most challenging and creative form of communication to keep staff more involved in their work.
- The entrepreneurial conversation produces the greatest intangible rewards because of the sense of accomplishment it engenders. Employees will be motivated to stay longer when encouraged to concentrate on long-term gains and goals.

- The entrepreneurial conversation builds the strongest bonds among colleagues, making their day-to-day work more enjoyable and satisfying.

Keep the following concepts in mind when using entrepreneurial conversations to develop entrepreneurial-minded employees:

Hire People Who Are Eager to Learn

Research shows that people who like to learn make the best employees. Think about it. People who enjoy acquiring new skills will be good at asking the right questions, listening for answers, and developing solutions to problems. Since the entrepreneurial conversation involves give-and-take, employees who are eager to learn are more likely to thrive in the workplace.

The pace of work in every industry today is faster, the expectations of clients and customers are higher, and the competition is tougher. Management must make certain that employees have up-to-date computer and communication skills, including Web-based applications and innovations not yet imagined. New employees must be brought up to speed and current employees must continue training. Only those willing to learn will be able to keep up with the increased demands.

Learning is essential to your entire workforce as the competition changes, markets expand, new products are developed, and people move within your organization. Employees who learn the fastest will provide success for both your organization and for themselves.

Use Positive Reinforcement

One hundred years of research could not be clearer in demonstrating that with people, dogs and just about every living creature, positive reinforcement is a far more powerful influence on behavior than negative reinforcement. When employees are engaged in entrepreneurial conversations with their managers, they benefit from the give-and-take of the open dialogue and from being treated like the valuable assets they are.

Add positive feedback into this mix through praise and respect, and your employees will respond by working creatively with their colleagues to forge new solutions to old problems. Never underestimate the value of praise, which is the most positive reinforcer of behavior known.

Don't get us wrong. A generous bonus check or raise is a great motivator. But motivation comes not just from monetary rewards, which everyone likes, but from the praise it represents. Positive feedback can take many forms besides money, including giving praise, creating milestones to provide a feeling of accomplishment, and rewarding good work with a new title, increased responsibilities, or a bigger office. Recognizing individuals in front of others for their strong performances helps people feel good about themselves.

Many old-school managers tend to use negative reinforcements such as making threats, instilling fear, reducing pay, or insulting and humiliating staff members. Negative reinforcements are potent motivators—but only for the short term. Their effects wear off, usually leaving a residue of bad feelings. Plus they won't have nearly the same impact the next time they are used.

Since long-term relationships are a boon to businesses, and since the entrepreneurial conversation is a long-term process, the only sensible course of action for the manager is to focus on positive reinforcements with the staff members he hopes will be equally long term.

Build Long-Term Relationships with Your Staff

Because entrepreneurial conversations are centered on long-term goals, rewards to the entrepreneurial staff, including compensation and recognition, should also reflect this long-term objective. A long-term focus argues for paying bonuses to employees who come up with new and better ideas, or who eagerly take on more responsibility.

Most importantly, emphasizing long-term relationships makes a case for giving incentives and recognition to employees who master the entrepreneurial conversation and use it to build equally long-term internal and external relationships that are valuable to the organization.

Successful entrepreneurs often give their employees a stake in the business, which can create a strong desire for business success among staff. This type of investment will also foster longer-term commitments from employees who want to see their investment of time and energy rewarded through some form of profit sharing.

Encourage Your Staff to Build Long-Term Relationships with Your Customers

Virtually every business is built on revenue from a relatively small group of important customers. The usual rule of thumb is that 20 percent of your clientele will account for 80 percent of your profits, a relationship that holds true from fast food restaurants on Main Street to stock brokerage firms on Wall Street. Professional service companies such as law firms, accounting firms and advertising agencies often have an even higher concentration of revenue from a few key clients.

We know of one major consulting firm that received more than half its revenue in recent years from one client, a European-based bank.

When Chrysler Corporation moved its advertising from True North Communications to Omnicom in 2000, it was estimated that True North would lose 9 percent of its total sales and one-third of its profits, signaling to everyone how essential the Chrysler account had been.

Small and start-up businesses are often totally dependent on one or two clients. The commitment from a single prospective customer is frequently what gives an entrepreneur the push to start her own business. Once the business is established, the entrepreneur must insure that this first client is kept happy at any cost, even as she works to develop new clients and lessen her dependence on her initial customer.

Existing clients represent not only your current base, but your potential for future growth. Even the giant on-line retailer Amazon.com, with millions of shoppers, reported that in 2000, returning customers accounted for 78 percent of all income. A study of on-line retailers by Bain & Co. and Mainspring found that the average purchase size grows with returning customers. The study reported that fifth purchases are, on average, 40 percent larger than first purchases, and that tenth purchases are generally 80 percent larger than first purchases.

All customers and orders are good, but long-term relationships that produce the reliable, bedrock revenue that keeps your business in business are the most important relationships your company maintains. Replacing an important client or customer, if it is even possible, carries a huge cost in terms of making increased sales calls and using valuable time that could be spent on servicing established customers.

When you focus on engaging in entrepreneurial conversations with your staff, then you will begin to see your employees using the same skills to maintain essential client relationships. There is nothing magical or mysterious about it. You will simply be marshaling the force of the entrepreneurial conversation.

Eliminate Wasteful Turnover

Nothing is more expensive and wasteful than staff turnover. Because it is hard to estimate the cost of turnover to an organization, most managers seem to shrug, complain about the inconvenience it causes, and hire a replacement.

To be fair, not all turnover is bad. Sometimes a marginal person decides to move on, or a strong employee has become bored and needs a new challenge that is best provided at another company. Some organizational renewal is a good thing, but generally turnover is an unwelcome phenomenon.

The major causes of turnover include employees who no longer find their work challenging, individuals who see little future in their current jobs, or workers who believe they have been treated inequitably on some issue—frequently, but not always, money.

It is difficult to estimate the actual expense of turnover because it has many hidden costs. You cannot easily determine how effective a new staff member will be or what a departed employee's positive influences were on others within the organization. The cost of hiring and training replacements, or the damage to the organization's internal and external relationships is equally hard to gauge. It is also easy to overlook the value of training that veterans give to rookies in the course of everyday business, or the possibility that the person's replacement won't work out and you'll have to start interviewing all over again. Whatever you may think the cost of turnover is, it is probably much greater.

When turnover is reduced and the average staff member gains experience, managers need to spend less time doing introductory training. Staff stability leads to more efficient communications and an increase in entrepreneurial conversations, which in turn helps to streamline operations and keep costs down. Most importantly, when costs decrease within an organization, revenues increase—all in all, a very happy outcome!

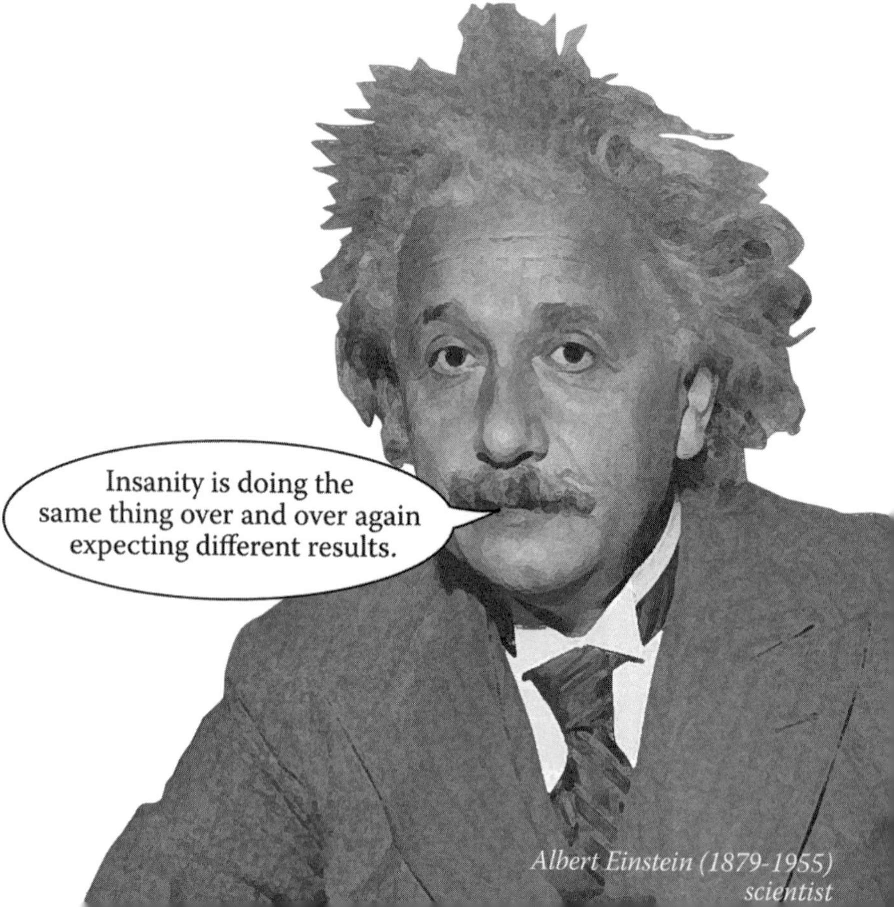

Albert Einstein (1879-1955)
scientist

Be a Coach, Not Just a Boss

The entrepreneurial manager needs to act like a coach, not just a boss. A coach is more than a simple supervisor. A coach is someone with greater experience who can help the staff develop better communication skills and a stronger commitment to work.

Think about a sports team and the place a coach has in building a successful season by understanding the individual players as well as the team dynamics. This includes considering individual attitudes and motivation, as well as fundamental talents and fitness for playing particular positions on the team.

If you want to be an entrepreneurial manager, think of yourself as a coach whose goal is success for you as well as for your team of employees. You are a mentor and a source of inspiration. Share your expertise so your staff can help your clients make better use of your products or services. Encourage creative thinking and be an advocate for your division with your own bosses.

Establish attainable but ambitious goals so your employees' ambitions are reinforced. Remember that entrepreneurial staff members prefer challenges. You'll soon realize that your bosses and your company's customers will appreciate the results as much as you do.

The Entrepreneurial Manager
Fosters an Entrepreneurial Company

When management stresses that the company's product or service is an important tool in helping their clients improve business or solve a problem, they have taken a huge step toward understanding the power of the entrepreneurial conversation. Most clients want to increase profits, revenue or market share; others may have more specific concerns such as reducing employee turnover, increasing average order size, or speeding up service times. The entrepreneurial manager who encourages his company to put the client's interests first, makes it much easier to sell his company's products.

- To sell its network hardware and software to businesses, Cisco Systems provides free workshops for executives from both existing and potential clients on how to use the Internet to help their businesses. Cisco never even makes a pitch for its hardware, knowing that clients must first see how the Internet can work for them.
- To sell its payroll accounting services to corporations, ADP not only provides an estimate of the cost savings to the company but argues that it makes fewer mistakes than company accountants and this makes the company's employees much happier.

- To sell computers and computer peripherals to small and mid-size companies, CDW Computer Centers moved away from the Internet and print catalogs to rely on more than 1,000 telephone account representatives. CDW understands that its customers want personal, knowledgeable and immediate service, not just a low price, so every account is assigned an individual representative. The results have been spectacular. Between 1995 and 2000, sales and profits rose an average of 40 percent per year. During the same period, average order size increased from $685 to $1,049, and repeat business increased to more than 80 percent of sales.

Create a Setting for Success

A good entrepreneurial manager will create an environment in which staff will have positive interactions with each other and with their bosses. Here are some suggestions that will allow entrepreneurial conversations to proliferate:

- *Be available to your staff.* Keep your door and mind open. Managers usually close their doors so their employees can't hear what's being discussed. Staff members understand this gesture, and it fuels their paranoia. They suspect you're talking about them, planning to replace them, selling the company, or reorganizing your department. Because these thoughts touch on our basic fears about being rejected, they prevent employees from thinking about more important issues, such as having entrepreneurial conversations with clients and each other.

- *Schedule regular informal staff meetings where any and all issues can be raised.* There is no better way for managers to demonstrate that they are not harboring secrets than to be open to discussing any issue publicly. Preparation, however, is required. Most managers can discern in advance what issues are likely to arise. And the wise ones have their answers prepared around their employees' real issues. We once witnessed a manager in a staff meeting in which she refused to discuss half the topics that were raised. These topics included a potential sale of the company, employee benefits, and a rumored change in compensation systems. She avoided addressing her employees' real issues and, as a result, her meeting did more harm than good.

- *Share as much information as possible.* Keeping your employees informed about your company's plans as well as its products is an important way to ensure that your conversations with them will focus on the real issues. When your employees are in the dark, they are likely to be nervous about the company and will feel uncomfortable about contributing openly on how to improve service or products.

- *Interact with your staff beyond meetings.* Bowling leagues are nice, but they're not essential for the entrepreneurial manager. Creating a good environment in the office is more effective and less time consuming, and it carries less risk to your fingers. Keep your attitude open and the atmosphere relaxed. Just talk to people. David Packard, the founder of Hewlett-Packard, called it "management by walking around." Talking to people at the elevator, by the water cooler, or just walking around leads to some of the best interactions between workers and bosses. And remember to listen, listen, listen.

- *Train your staff to keep their skills sharp.* Learning is central to entrepreneurial organizations and must remain a priority in your interactions with employees. Remember that people who like to learn make great staff members, and they take to entrepreneurial conversations very quickly. To keep people learning and to reinforce that you embrace learning, the organization must promote education at every opportunity. Reimburse staff for outside training courses, bring in guest speakers, and have discussions about readings that management has distributed. Encourage employees to train each other by assigning topics for presentations at staff meetings. Training is worth the time and expense because employees learn new skills, feel more prepared, and recognize that they are valued.

- ***Don't misinterpret body language.*** Employees often feel nervous about meeting with their managers, but it is your job to understand the nonverbal cues of a conversation and make your staff comfortable while speaking with you. Uncomfortable people respond in different ways. Some will become agitated and speak too quickly. Others may become stilted and quiet. Remember that this is how they feel about meeting with you, but it's not necessarily the way they feel about you. If your attitude is non-judgmental and relaxed, and you are focused on your employees' real issues, you are half way there.

- ***Help your staff master their own entrepreneurial conversations.*** If your employees understand what you're doing in an entrepreneurial conversation, they will learn how to increase their own communication skills. Encourage your staff to apply entrepreneurial conversations to their internal relationships with you and each other, as well in their external relationships with clients and customers.

Share this book with your employees and have a discussion about this chapter in particular. Arrange for outside experts to evaluate the first impressions your employees make, so you are not performing the dual role of stage mother and manager.

Sales Managers Have Special Entrepreneurial Goals

When you work primarily in sales, your focus is geared toward very specific and often measurable objectives. Sales managers who want to instill an entrepreneurial spirit among their sales staff will have to engage in entrepreneurial conversations that add certain elements to the basic entrepreneurial conversation. Please also be sure to read *Chapter 6: The Entrepreneurial Salesperson*, so you'll know how we encourage members of your staff to become more entrepreneurial on their own terms.

Establish Rewards that Are Focused on the Long Term

Since entrepreneurial selling is focused on long-term goals, the rewards to the staff, including compensation, should reflect that same long-term objective. This argues for higher fixed compensation, bonuses for new client development, and incentive compensation plans that are based on quarterly or even yearly performances rather than on short-term monthly earnings.

Instead of monitoring the sheer number of sales calls, you should track the number of customers a salesperson is engaging in entrepreneurial conversations. It is these calls, not the volume of calls, that will lead to the largest number of long-term clients.

Reward your staff for obtaining professional training. Giving a title such as Senior Salesperson to reflect additional training can be a significant positive reinforcement. Raising fixed compensation for a salesperson who has received additional training, or increasing the commission rate based on the amount of training, demonstrates that your organization values learning new skills.

Most importantly, management should recognize in front of others the salesperson who obtains training, does extensive research before meeting with a client, or engages in any activity that promotes the use of entrepreneurial conversations.

Encourage Your Salespeople to
Build Success for Their Clients

We knew an old-school manager who constantly asked his salespeople, "What did you do for me today?" The question the entrepreneurial sales manager should ask is, "What did you do today to build success for your clients?" A sales force that is focused on making your product or service more valuable to your clients is a sales force committed to long-term, mutually beneficial, entrepreneurial relationships.

The strongest motivation for any salesperson is client service. If the salesperson sees his first duty as serving his clients and has worked diligently and honestly to do just that, then missing a monthly goal, or having to listen to the ranting of a weak sales manager will not pull him down into a morass of negative feelings. Focusing on client service will motivate and energize your sales staff, which in turn will make them more appealing to your clients.

Establish an Environment to Provide Superior Customer Service

It's the sales manager's job to encourage staff members to offer the best service to customers. Ways to accomplish this include providing technical support to your sales staff from others in the company, making yourself available to meet with clients, and allowing salespeople to spend as much time with clients as necessary.

We worked with Bill, an experienced, organized and highly motivated sales manager after he learned the advantages of building a staff of entrepreneurial salespeople. Bill found that his appreciation for his own job increased as his sales force developed their own entrepreneurial skills.

"I found myself spending more time developing solutions for customers, which I enjoyed," claimed Bill, "and less time having unpleasant interactions with salespeople about how they should be making more calls."

Wisdom
of the
Entrepreneurial
Masters
Dick Merians

Dick Merians, the founder and president of Hygrade Logistics, a nationwide trucking and logistics solutions company, is a tall and elegant man. He is hardly someone you would assume founded a shipping company in the 1960s by buying a single truck. But he is a man whose entrepreneurial conversations are the cornerstone of his business and managerial success.

Dick claims that his first lesson in entrepreneurship was learning that there's always someone who will undercut your price to get the business. "So I realized," explains Dick, "that I had to choose a market segment that had a greater degree of entry difficulty and specialization so there would be less competition." After engaging in entrepreneurial conversations with many people in various industries, Dick decided to limit his trucking company to furniture deliveries.

"There is a real focus on quality in the furniture delivery business," Dick says, "mostly because of the high risk of damage and because companies care greatly about providing friendly and prompt service to their customers." As he learned more about his customers' real issues, Dick realized that furniture dealers were losing millions of dollars on inefficiently run warehouses where their goods were often misplaced and damaged. If he could help his customers manage their warehouses more efficiently, Dick felt he would be providing a new and valuable service.

Dick made a proposal to a New York department store to do just that. At a time when furniture dealers were just beginning to use computers to solve their problems, Dick's company designed, built, installed and managed the first furniture warehouse computer system. It was a huge success and vastly increased the ease and speed of handling inventory. Soon Hygrade Logistics was managing warehouses throughout the country.

Dick's business soon grew into a large and diversified company that included trucking, software production and warehouse management. Because the size and scope of Hygrade Logistics became more than one person could manage, Dick used his knowledge and managerial skills to build an entrepreneurial workforce.

Dick restructured his company to turn his employees into individual entrepreneurs. Hygrade is now decentralized, with managers who have the discretion to make their own decisions within clearly established boundaries. All of Dick's staff members, including the administrative employees, are paid incentives based on both company profitability and the results of a customer service report card that is mailed to every client once a year. "This provides a powerful incentive for success," says Dick.

Hygrade also pays its employees as well as, if not better than, its competition, so the package of compensation, incentives and benefits has created a staff with little turnover and long-term commitment to the company. "My employees also get along much better with each other since I restructured," says Dick. "They feel they are part of a team, working together for a common goal. Even my managers talk to each other more frequently. They're not so focused on internal competitiveness. Now they're more interested in competing with other storage and delivery companies." This entrepreneurial spirit gives Hygrade Logistics staff members the in-depth customer knowledge, continuity, service skills and good relationships that keep their clients satisfied year after year.

Dick Merians is a great example of a manager who engages in entrepreneurial conversations with both his customers and employees to build a successful, entrepreneurial company. Dick sums up his thinking this way: "Everyone knows that satisfied employees lead to satisfied customers, but I have also learned that satisfied customers lead to satisfied employees."

6 the entrepreneurial Salesperson

"We are all salespeople."
—*Charles Schwab, founder
of brokerage firm Charles Schwab &
Company*

No matter what we do for a living, we all spend considerable time of every day trying to convince others to accept our individual points of view. Take one full day to listen to yourself and others. See how many of your conversations consist of selling someone on an idea or a way of looking at a situation. Chances are you'll realize there's little else but selling going on all around you.

When you try to talk your way out of a traffic

ticket, you're selling. When you attempt to convince your children to do their chores, you're selling. When they insist that they have more important tasks to do, such as their homework, they're trying to convince you to buy their argument. When people call you up and invite you to a party, they're selling the desirability of their company—and yours.

So please read this chapter, even if you don't define your basic activity as sales. Similarly, you should read *Chapter 5: The Entrepreneurial Manager* whether you are a manager or not. Because if you are not a manager, Chapter 5 will show you what your boss should be accomplishing.

Sales Is Not a Four-Letter Word

Despite the fact that over fifteen million people in the U.S. earn their living through sales, and the rest of us employ salesmanship to convince our students, patients, children or others that our ideas are sound, people still think that selling implies getting others to do something they don't really want to do, to buy something they don't really need, or to take an action that is clearly against their own best interests.

This prejudice against selling is overwhelming, despite the fact that people who can think, listen and speak effectively in order to deliver the resources their organizations need—more clients, more investors, more viewers, more patients—are essentially selling. We know of no MBA program in the United States that teaches selling. In fact, one of the largest business publishers in the world said it would buy this book if we deleted the word "sales" throughout the manuscript. We tried various other options such as "you-know-what," "the 's' word," and "resource development science." But selling is omnipresent and everyone does it, so we bid farewell to that effort—and to that particular publisher.

This unfortunate view defines selling as a short-term interaction in which one person wins and the other one loses. It ignores the give-and-take of a mutually productive entrepreneurial conversation that builds a long-term relationship.

Selling Is Ubiquitous

Many people believe that certain professionals, such as artists or research scientists, have little to do with selling or entrepreneurship. But their success often depends on their ability to sell. Artists must think about finding their best audience and they must speak to the right people to recruit their aid in writing about, showing and buying their work. How well artists present themselves and their art may determine their success in finding and building a market for their work.

We may also assume that astrophysicists or biochemists are consumed only by their research, but their ability to be successful involves more than the quality of their work. They must present their research to journal editors to publish it, foundations and universities to fund it, and their colleagues to accept it.

Everyone is, in some form or another, selling. And everyone is, essentially, working in some kind of entrepreneurial manner.

Therefore, the art of the entrepreneurial conversation and learning how to think, listen and speak like a successful entrepreneur can benefit anyone—teachers, managers, musicians, artists, accountants, waitresses, physicians and lawyers—not just salespeople or entrepreneurs who are starting their own businesses.

As long as you and everyone you'll be speaking to in your personal or professional life has something to give or something to take, it's best to understand how thinking, listening and speaking effectively can benefit everyone involved. Entrepreneurial conversations are the key to your success.

The Old School of Selling Has Let Out; Class Is In Session for the Entrepreneurial Conversation

Entrepreneurs build success when they secure the best resources to start and grow their businesses. Salespeople build success when they recruit clients, distributors, partners, accounts, or whatever else will generate revenue and growth for their companies. Whether your company sells tangibles or intangibles, or serves businesses or consumers, your success rests on your ability to make the connection between your product and meeting your clients' needs. And the best way to accomplish this goal is to engage your customers in entrepreneurial conversations.

The reality is that most salespeople are taught what we call old-school techniques that actually prevent them from making sales or holding mutually productive entrepreneurial conversations.

The old-school constructs of a sale as a manipulation rest on an outdated business model of big, largely self-sufficient companies. But today, successful companies outsource rather than hire, lease rather than buy, and rent rather than invent. Delivering quality products and services to their customers quickly is a priority.

If you want to find out how to unlock the potential of the entrepreneurial conversation for you and your organization's benefit, as well as for the benefit of everyone with whom you come in contact, keep reading. And get ready to power up both your career and your sales success.

You Simply Have More Competition than Previous Generations

Around the turn of the 20th century, when selling methods were first analyzed and defined, business people had very few means of exchanging information. Advertising was limited primarily to newspapers, magazines, mail-order catalogs, and the sides of buildings or horse-drawn delivery wagons.

Salespeople in those days were employed as mouthpieces to deliver preprogrammed messages as canned and as static as a billboard slogan. In the late 1800s and early 1900s, businesses such as the Singer Sewing Machine Company and Metropolitan Life grew quite handsomely by using salespeople who were trained to deliver verbatim scripts to their prospects. The salesperson's job was to find the potential clients, recite the message, solicit interest, and write the order.

Today there are many new avenues of communication: television commercials, radio advertisements, telephone pitches, direct mail solicitations, interactive Web sites and e-mail, to name just a few. But at the same time that the explosion in communication technologies has made people easier to reach, it has also deval-ued the art of communication. Today's average sales call is shorter, gets to the point faster and is often interrupted by pagers, cell phones and staff members. Perhaps we are simply overloaded with the barrage of information, or the contact is just too easy and informal. Whatever the reason, in this fast-paced business world many people seem to ignore messages in any form, or, at the least, respond to them lackadaisically.

A salesperson needs to be visible in this blitz of information sharing and selling. The good news is that acquiring the skills of the entrepreneurial conversation will help tremendously. If you are diligent about your research and timely in getting back to people, you will stand out as being knowledgeable, credible and dependable. If you are patient, rather than pushy, your ability to listen will enable you to explore mutually beneficial ways to work together. And, if you are more concerned about your customers' needs than yours when you speak, they will be more open with you. The entrepreneurial conversation is a powerful tool that will make you stand out from the crowd—and the modern-day rush.

The Eight Major Myths of Old-School Selling

To know where you're going, you usually have to know where you've been. What we call old-school sales techniques usually encourage salespeople to focus on short-term goals, but this only creates a poorly trained sales staff that's in a hurry. Most salespeople exposed to this type of encouragement will fail miserably and won't be with a company for long. Old-school techniques fail to provide a formula for success because they fail to encourage salespeople who understand the power of the entrepreneurial conversation. Let's take a look at these old-school myths and see what they actually accomplish.

Myth # 1:
Selling Is a Psychological Process

This approach has been around for many years in many guises. One of the first books on selling, *Read's Salesmanship*, was published in 1915. Author Harlan Eugene Read identified the psychological selling steps as Awakening Interest, Arousing Desire, Compelling Action, Asking for the Order, and Answering Objections. While the names of the steps have changed, the basic concepts have remained the same.

E.K. Strong, in his 1925 book, *The Psychology of Selling*, reduced selling to the four-step "AIDA" model of Attention, Interest, Desire and Action. In 1971, Jack Huttig wrote *Psycho-Sales-Analysis*, in which he described the six steps up the golden stairway to successful selling: Prospecting, Contacting, Interest, Preference, Proposal and Close. In their 1991 book, *Professional Selling*, Gary Soldow and Gloria Thomas present the AIDA model all over again.

Old-school sales techniques focus on using methods such as getting agreements to specific points before asking for the order, or teaching salespeople programmed "mini-scripts" to guide them through the rigid steps of psychological selling. Some old-school writers urge salespeople to focus on the client's body language by interpreting posture, leg position and eye contact as indicators of a person's psychological attitude.

We agree that everything human beings think, say and do is part of a psychological process. The problem with this out-dated approach is that there is no single identifiable sequence that always leads to a sale. Clients and customers often move directly to purchasing; other times they go through a long, often repetitive process before they can make the decision to buy.

The notion that all salespeople can maneuver customers up a golden staircase to a sale is simply false. By thinking clearly about your client's real issues, and by listening carefully so you can create mutually beneficial ways of working together, you are far more likely to make a sale.

Myth #2:
Selling Is a Manipulative Process

We all know salespeople whose approach to selling is to manipulate or push the client into an agreement. This is a type of "reverse psychology" technique in which a salesperson makes clients feel so inadequate they must buy to prove they are worthy human beings.

Another maneuver is to place clients in a peer pressure situation so they buy to be a part of the group or to make buying an ego-boosting experience. Still another manipulative tactic is to become the client's friend so he wants to please you by purchasing your service or product. One favorite ploy that has been around for decades and shows the level to which this strategy can descend is to "accidentally" roll a pen across the table to the client just before asking him to sign the order.

The shortcomings of this manipulative approach are legion, and their consequences have led to even more books and theories. For example, there are techniques for "handling objections," when a customer expresses reasons for not buying a product, or "managing buyer's remorse," when a client feels guilty about having agreed to spend so much money on an item.

We don't believe that selling or interacting with people is about using manipulative techniques. Manipulation is phony and is quickly exposed. Once your customers become aware of the trick, they will never buy from you again. You won't need fake techniques if you are having entrepreneurial conversations and addressing the other person's real issues.

Every truth leads to
another truth.

Ralph Waldo Emerson
(1803-1882)
philosopher, poet

Myth #3:
Selling Is a Consultative Process

Because of the shortcomings of the traditional psychological and manipulative processes, some managers turn their salespeople into so-called "consultants." Proponents of this approach include Mack Hanan, who outlined this concept in his 1985 book, *Consultative Selling,* and Tony Alessandra and Rick Barrera, who wrote *Collaborative Selling* in 1993. These approaches basically follow the AIDA model, while trying to give the client the impression that salespeople are really only "consultants" who need to collect information about the client's business.

This is actually a version of the manipulative process model. The consultative technique relies on the assumption that potential clients like talking about their businesses and enjoy people who are good listeners, which is true, but this one-sided approach doesn't focus on the client's real issues and never leads to a true conversation.

Salespeople trained in this consultative method learn to repeat customers' words back to them to reinforce the decision to buy. Consultative salespeople are rarely influenced by what they have "dutifully" listened to, and the proposal they make is exactly the same as the one offered by the traditional, non-consultative, salesperson.

We have both spent years in the broadcast media industry—Ed as the owner of two different radio companies and Michael as a sales expert—and we have seen hundreds of radio and television advertising salespeople who present themselves to their clients as "consultants." Yet we have never seen even one of those "consultants" change his proposal based on what he heard during the so-called "consultation" with the client.

Wearing the guise of a consultant is largely a fraud to make the client feel less pressured as a buyer and to make the salesperson feel better about selling. Eventually the client realizes the ruse, comes to resent this time-consuming game, and the relationship breaks down. The true dialogue inherent in the entrepreneurial conversation will lead to an open exchange of information.

Myth #4:
Set High Performance Goals

Absurdly high performance goals are a proven de-motivator. Managers should set goals high enough to encourage salespeople to work hard, but the goals should always be attainable. Constantly failing to reach a sales goal is a sure path to demoralization.

The quota system is simply a variant of high-performance goals that carries the clear threat of termination should the quota not be reached. Failing constantly can create poor staff morale, which in turn leads to poor sales.

Although all entrepreneurial conversations will not lead to sales, all sales accomplished through entrepreneurial conversations will likely lead to long-term, mutually beneficial relationships with clients.

Myth #5:
Make Zillions of Sales Calls

Some sales managers recognize that sales is, to a large extent, a numbers game. They like to believe that every breathing human being is a prospect. We've seen sales managers point out the window to a street or hold up the phone book and tell their staff, "Here are your future customers!"

This is not only false, it is, ultimately, self-defeating.

Calling on inappropriate prospects and getting nowhere, except being shown the door, is a fast path to demoralization. After hearing a long string of "no's" or failing to engage prospects in any aspect of an entrepreneurial conversation, you will begin to believe that your product or service is appropriate to no one.

If someone tells you that everyone is a prospect, ask yourself, "Am I a prospect?" or "Does virtually everyone I know use this product or service?" We suppose that if you're selling soap the answer might be yes. But then the next question would still be, "Where are my efforts best spent to get the maximum results?" The answer would lead you to focus on certain clients, such as a handful of wholesalers or retailers who have the greatest need for your product—and the greatest ability to generate revenue for your company.

A sales management system that sets a quota for the number of calls made, encourages the salesperson to make a large number of calls without being prepared or able to commit the time to build long-term relationships with clients. The quality of each sales call is much more important than the sheer number. An entrepreneurial conversation takes a lot of preparation and a great deal of discussion with the customer. It may also take several meetings to develop a relationship and a plan for working together, but in the long run, the results will be far more substantial.

Myth #6:
Try to Get Orders as Quickly as Possible

"Close, close, close," is the battle cry for many old-school sales managers. Pressuring the salesperson to get the order as quickly as possible (certainly before the end of the month) only short-circuits the entrepreneurial conversation.

Closing too quickly encourages the salesperson to spend as little time as possible learning from the client and prevents the development of a mutually beneficial plan for working together. Turning salespeople into "closing specialists" reinforces every negative stereotype about salespeople and signals to your clients that your company is hard to work with and inflexible.

Engaging in entrepreneurial conversations will take more time but will bring better results.

Myth #7:
Compensate Solely on Performance

Compensation based largely on performance is used as a surrogate management tool by old-school managers because it constantly reminds salespeople that by closing quickly, they will soon see a reward in their paycheck. It's important to make the incentives for the salesperson match the interests of the organization, but money is usually only one of many possible motivators.

Managers who focus exclusively on incentive pay or commissions usually give their sales staff a very short-term perspective. The best relationships with clients and customers are the ones that are built through entrepreneurial conversations because they are well-founded, mutually beneficial and long-term.

Myth #8:
Training Is a Necessary Evil

Old-school managers believe that a certain amount of training is necessary because the company can't send out completely ignorant salespeople, but they also see training as evil, because it takes time and therefore reduces the number of calls a salesperson can make. These managers think training is an expensive distraction from making more calls and closing more sales. However, not only is knowledge important to being a successful entrepreneurial salesperson, but valuing learning is a powerful attribute of successful salespeople.

Tap into the Entrepreneurial Spirit

Even if you're stuck with an old-school manager who believes in the outdated myths of selling, you can overcome many of the obstacles placed in your path by employing the power of the entrepreneurial conversation with clients and customers.

Understand What a Sales Call Is

A sales call should always be an entrepreneurial conversation. By understanding the power of thinking, listening and speaking you will be able to develop possibilities, agree on specific courses of action, and achieve mutually beneficial results with your clients. When you focus on engaging in entrepreneurial conversations, you are doing far more than making a single sale; you are building long-term, satisfying relationships with clients.

The Customer Is Still *Always Right*

This is an age-old rule we agree with whole-heartedly. The fundamental reality of the entrepreneurial sales conversation is set by your customers. The real issues are their issues. The problems that need to be resolved are their problems. Ignoring their issues or problems is fatal to your goal of achieving a mutually beneficial outcome.

Ignoring your customers' concerns tells them that you don't value what they think, or that you may not even be listening, a perception that can damage even the most carefully crafted atmosphere you have created for your entrepreneurial conversation. If your customers' problems are not addressed in your conversations, these unhandled issues will always stand in the way of an agreement to work together.

When the customer raises an issue, it must be dealt with immediately and resolved explicitly. If your customer cares about speed of delivery and you can't accommodate the request, say so. Don't try to talk the customer into accepting a lower price if that still won't guarantee prompt delivery. And if your customer says your delivery wasn't timely, don't argue or make excuses. Find out what went wrong and fix it. And if you can't fix it, tell your customer that you will not be able to improve on delivery in the future. Honesty is *still* the best policy.

Use the Power of Existing Relationships

The existing relationships that companies have with their customers is what keeps them in business. End these relationships and you end the company. Yet many companies take existing relationships for granted, focusing instead on finding new and bigger accounts. Established relationships require entrepreneurial conversations just as much as new prospects. Here are three questions to ask yourself about the value of existing relationships:

- *What is an existing relationship worth and what would it cost to replace?* It's much more than you think if you add in the time spent making new contacts until a new relationship is built with another client.
- *How do you maintain existing relationships with clients?* You keep having entrepreneurial conversations with them!
- *When do you end an existing relationship with a client?* When you can no longer work wholeheartedly on the client's behalf or when your services or products can no longer produce a good result for your customer.

Many salespeople feel rewarded by the process of "landing a new account." This psychological high often makes salespeople focus on "getting accounts" instead of "keeping accounts."

Engaging in entrepreneurial conversations with existing customers can deepen your understanding of their needs, develop new ways to meet their goals, and keep that relationship productive for many years to come.

Don't Play Games by Sizing Up Clients

The tendency of salespeople to "size up" prospects seems to be an almost unavoidable occupational hazard. Many bored salespeople enjoy the game of forming an instant judgment of a customer and then seeing how accurate their verdict turns out to be. This game almost always results in "profiling" people based on characteristics such as their age, gender, race or clothing. This steers the prospect to choices that confirm the salesperson's initial judgment, often leading to a less than optimal outcome.

A typical example is the car salesperson who guides blue jeans-clad prospects to low-priced vehicles, even after they ask to see higher-priced cars, because he doesn't believe that someone in jeans will actually buy an expensive car. Obviously he hasn't had many rock stars or founders of "dot.com" businesses as clients.

In his 1924 *Textbook of Salesmanship*, Frederic A. Russell described this process, along with the risks of ignoring qualified prospects. Russell quotes William Maxwell, vice president of sales for Thomas A. Edison's company:

...the greatest and most common sin of salesmen is their belief in their ability to 'pick winners.' You walk into a Fifth Avenue store. The salesman sizes you up for a live one or a dead one. It doesn't matter what you are. It only matters how the salesman happens to classify you, and after he has done so—read your character, as he probably calls it—nothing you can do will change his opinion of you. If he sized you up as a dead one, but you nonetheless buy something, he is more likely to conclude that you were embarrassed by his aloof attitude and made the purchase to save your face. Almost never will he admit that he sized you up wrongly. I don't believe in character-reading salesmen. My experience has been that character reading is more frequently an alibi for not getting an order than an aid in getting one.

The sizing-up game results in dissatisfied and disappointed clients and a salesperson without a sale. Your task as a salesperson is to have an entrepreneurial conversation with potential customers, not to play a game that tests your initial judgment of them.

Build on Long-term Relationships when Selling Directly to Consumers

Many people argue that the techniques we decry, such as pushing the client to buy immediately, actually work for consumer selling, despite the fact that they also erode trust in the relationship.

Michael remembers watching a salesperson in a jewelry store near a Navy base. The majority of the store's sales were to sailors who came in with their fiancées to buy engagement or wedding rings. The salesperson was a well-turned-out woman in her late thirties who wore lots of expensive jewelry. Her technique was to use embarrassment to manipulate her customers into spending more than they could afford.

Holding the small diamond ring that the sailor had picked out next to the large diamond on her own finger, she would say, "See how much better the bigger diamond looks? I've worn this ring every day for fifteen years. I'm so glad my husband didn't skimp on it."

She told Michael that this technique worked almost every time, failing only when the bride-to-be intervened and said that she didn't want the larger diamond. The salesperson's rationale for using this technique was simple. "Virtually all these sailors live in this community for only a short time," she explained. "I'll make only one sale to them and I want to make a good one."

Indeed, she did make many good sales, but she left these sailors feeling manipulated and pressured into spending more than they wanted. Certainly those who stayed in the naval base community did not return to this store for anniversary gifts.

This short-term rather than long-term view is what drives the use of manipulative techniques in consumer selling. If the salesperson isn't interested in building a strong relationship with a customer, then he doesn't care about destroying long-term possibilities by using manipulative sales techniques.

Many retailers use this long-term, customer-oriented approach effectively. Nordstrom department stores, for example, are famous for training salespeople to give the customer as many options as possible, but not to push the reluctant buyer into making a purchase. The sales staff is encouraged to hold items for twenty-four hours in order to give the customer ample time to make the decision to buy.

L.L. Bean and Land's End are known for excellent return policies and replacing products until their customers are satisfied. Clearly there is a connection between how these companies treat their customers and their continued business success and longevity.

Why wouldn't this approach work for every business?

The Entrepreneurial Conversation Levels the Playing Field

Many people believe that selling is a form of begging and that salespeople will be more effective if they see themselves as supplicants to the buyer. We don't believe that putting yourself at the feet of anyone else is the way to build a successful, long-term career—or successful long-term relationships with your clients.

The entrepreneurial conversation places the salesperson and the client on an equal footing so they're two professionals developing mutually beneficial ways of working together.

Many salespeople resent clients who talk down to them or treat them as if they were inferior. One example that stands out is Helen, an account representative for an advertising agency. Helen was a well-trained, capable, hardworking person who did a great job for her clients. But when it came to getting new clients, Helen always felt like a supplicant going to see the king. We accompanied Helen on a few sales calls and saw why she felt that way.

Helen had a book of flip charts that she placed on a prospect's desk and flicked through as she described her advertising agency. Pictures of the agency's production studio and headquarters were of little interest to the clients, who found Helen's presentation boring and a waste of time.

We counseled Helen to lose the charts and listen and speak so her clients discussed what her agency could do for them. Helen also realized that she had been misinterpreting the unspoken messages in her meetings by assuming that her potential clients were haughty when the poor souls were merely bored by her presentation. Helen's new approach is based on researching the company and the industry before her initial meeting, and focusing on uncovering the client's real issues and goals.

Helen's success rate has improved tremendously. More importantly, she now finds her conversations with clients enjoyable. By focusing on thinking, listening and speaking rather than relying on flip charts and a canned presentation, Helen has leveled the playing field. She now feels more professional and less like a supplicant in her meetings with prospective clients.

Avoid the Three Most Common Ways Salespeople Upset Clients

Old-school approaches to selling don't work because they ask for the impossible. They force sales staff members to behave in aggressive and manipulative ways that are uncomfortable for most people. Old-school sales techniques also demand that clients focus on the sales presentation, process all of the information, and buy the pitch all within a matter of minutes.

Having witnessed thousands of sales calls during our combined careers of over sixty years in management, education, sales and entrepreneurship, we have been able to identify the three most common ways salespeople upset clients. Learn to recognize these mistakes and you will realize why salespeople who engage in entrepreneurial conversations don't fall into these traps:

- ***Causing the client to have misleading expectations.*** It is very common for salespeople to "oversell" their products or services, promising features that can't be delivered. Salespeople may also demonstrate a level of extraordinary personal service for their clients, which later turns out to be extraordinary only by its brevity. This "over-selling" and "over-servicing" can falsely raise the client's expectations. When reality sets in and expectations cannot be met, clients invariably become upset and are reluctant to continue the relationship. Simple honesty and good service will almost always build long-term, positive transactions with clients.

- ***Preventing the client from accomplishing a goal.*** Most salespeople look forward to learning that their product or service has helped their clients significantly. But if the warehouse delivers the wrong item, it's useless. Salespeople have to focus on the clients' real issues in order to meet all of their clients' goals. They also must maintain good relationships with their colleagues in other divisions to make certain the clients are treated properly at all levels of service.

- *Failing to deliver bad news.* No one likes to deliver bad news, but bad news delivered late, or not at all, becomes worse news. We knew an election campaign manager who ordered a large printing of flyers for his candidate. Political campaigns, being of short duration, rely on timely deliveries. When the delivery date came and the printing job didn't, the campaign manager called the printer, who said, "Oh, I've been meaning to call you to say the job will be four days late." That was the last job the printer ever received from the manager, who went on to run many more political campaigns. If you give the bad news as soon as possible, you allow the greatest opportunity to negotiate an adjustment, which shows that you have the courage to be forthright.

Wisdom
of the
Entrepreneurial
Masters
Lloyd Weill

For 52 years, **Lloyd Weill** was a sales representative for manufacturers of women's designer clothing. Until he retired in 1999, Lloyd covered fourteen southern and southwestern states by plane, train and car. He displayed his goods in customers' stores, trade shows, merchandise marts, and in large rented hotel suites, called sample rooms. Lloyd was usually on the road twenty-six weeks each year. During the summers, his wife, Rusty, a schoolteacher, traveled with him.

Lloyd's entire career was spent developing an entrepreneurial attitude toward his job and working with customers to understand their needs and achieve their goals. His education as an entrepreneurial salesperson began when he started working in his father's haberdashery shop in Chicago. It was here that Lloyd learned how to present the goods properly, describe them effectively, and engage his customers in conversations about their needs. He discovered that the more he listened to his potential customers, the more comfortable they felt and the more he learned about their expectations.

When Lloyd decided to make selling a career, he went to work for an uncle who owned a dress manufacturing business. Before he would let Lloyd sell, his uncle made him work in every department of the company so that he knew the product, how it was made, and how the company operated. Lloyd's uncle was teaching him the value of being able to think like an entrepreneur by being knowledgeable and credible.

Lloyd eventually left his uncle's company to work as a salesperson for a line of women's designer clothing. "I loved selling," he says, "but the real keys to my success were my extensive knowledge about my products, about the store owners I called on, and the people who shopped in their stores." Lloyd also believes that his ability to solve problems was enormously useful. "I would help store owners find one dress in a certain size for an important customer. I would discover what was working in one store and pass that information along to my other clients."

He also realized that the way goods were presented was a major element in his business. "Products need to be presented with some romance," says Lloyd, who still looks dapper and somewhat formal, even in a polo shirt, khakis and sneakers. "You want your customers to enjoy their work, too." When Lloyd began visiting his dress shop clients, he learned the value of following a network of colleagues. He joined an informal group of New York-based women's clothing salesmen who handled the same territory and called themselves the "Southern Travelers." When Lloyd retired in 1999, he was the last remaining member of the original Southern Travelers still working.

"It was like a fraternity," Lloyd explains. "We were often in the same cities at the same time and displayed our goods at the same trade shows. Later, when merchandise marts came into being, we rented showrooms side-by-side." Lloyd and the Southern Travelers shared information on different contacts and ways to make customers more satis-fied with their services. "We really helped each other and shared our expertise," he says. "When one of us learned about a new trend in a color, or fabric or design from our clients and their customers, we discussed it so we could alert our manufacturers."

Lloyd also had a strong set of ethical stan-dards and a solid orientation toward doing right by his clients. For example, whenever Lloyd bought dresses for a customer who couldn't attend a trade show, he would buy fewer rather than too many dresses. "You never want to oversell the client," he explains. "I could always get them more goods later. You want to sell clients *into* business, not sell them *out of* business."

The indisputable lesson of Lloyd's career is that thinking, listening and speaking like a successful entrepreneur enabled him to build long-term success for his clients and himself. Lloyd was knowledgeable about his products and his customer's businesses. He was credible, honest and ethical. He always put his clients' needs above his own and he never over-promised. And, fundamentally, Lloyd was—and is—a likable person, who is genuinely interested in others, a patient listener and a caring colleague.

After fifty-two years on the road and two years of retirement, Lloyd is still in contact with his customers. "They became dear friends. I'm still in touch with many of them. The best part of my career was meeting and working with these people and helping us all be successful."

7 Mastering the Art of the entrepreneurial conversation

As you gain experience engaging in entrepreneurial conversations, you will achieve a level of mastery that will enable you to be even more effective. You will no longer try to get something from someone who will not receive anything in return. Nor will you be convincing people to do something they don't want to do. With the entrepreneurial conversation, your thinking, listening and speaking will always be focused on working with others to develop mutually beneficial long-term relationships.

We'd like to offer you some words of wisdom as you continue to develop your entrepreneurial skills.

There is no force so powerful as an idea whose time has come.

Victor Hugo (1802-1885)
author

Make Certain the Other Person Participates

A successful entrepreneurial conversation produces an agreement between two parties on a course of action. However, that course of action may not always be obvious, especially at the beginning of a meeting. It is the job of the entrepreneurial person to guide the discussion so that both parties participate in uncovering the real issues, proposing potential courses of action, evaluating those possibilities, and eventually narrowing them down to an agreed upon solution.

Creating Possibilities
Creates Mutual Participation

Your newly honed abilities to think, listen and speak effectively will enable you to draw the other person into the discussion. It is only through this dynamic dialogue that you will be able to bring up ideas and analyze them together and uncover the best possibilities for action.

This lively exchange of concepts goes by many different names. Advertising pioneer Alex Osborn coined the word "brainstorming" in his book *Applied Imagination*. Psychologist John S. Dacey called it "creative thinking." The prolific writer and scholar Edward deBono termed it "lateral thinking," and psychologist J. P. Guilford labeled it "divergent thinking."

We happen to call it "kicking ideas around," but no matter what it's labeled, it describes the process of creating as many possibilities as are imaginable. "Kicking ideas around" is integral to every entrepreneurial conversation. From the resulting list of possibilities will come the course of action that you and the other person will choose together. The more thorough the list, the more varied the possibilities will be and the more likely the two of you will find an approach that will produce your mutually desired results.

Some people think that kicking ideas around requires a large group of people (meeting in a secluded conference center, preferably near a sizable body of water) led by an expensive creative thinking expert. This can certainly work, but entrepreneurs rarely have the time for this type of group exercise. With the power of the entrepreneurial conversation firmly in your grasp, you can tease out mutually beneficial solutions from two people who are simply kicking ideas around.

Here are our guidelines to make kicking ideas around as productive as possible:

- *Avoid negative or positive comments.* Until you can complete the list of possible courses of action, don't pass judgments. Your goal is to produce the most varied inventory of ideas, regardless of how practical or realistic they are. Ideas beget other ideas, and an outlandish notion proposed by one person may trigger another to think of a workable concept. Most concepts that sound reasonable are solutions that have already been tried. Creative possibilities often sound improbable, impractical, silly or even funny. Don't be prejudiced! So until you begin to evaluate and rank the list of ideas, don't criticize or praise. Be open and be encouraging.

- *Appoint yourself the designated recorder.* No matter how certain you are that you'll remember key points, don't risk it. Take complete notes and write down every concept that evolves from your entrepreneurial conversations. Give every suggestion equal weight so the ideas keep flowing.
- *Graph your ideas.* Mix and match concepts along various dimensions. When marketing experts create names for new products, they design a grid to compare and combine all the possible nouns and adjectives. Being able to see different combinations of ideas graphically can lead to more possibilities and a more effective final course of action.

Possibilities Lead to Action

The forward momentum of creating possibilities together is exciting and productive for both parties. Conversations that hover endlessly in a cycle of excuses, explanations and debate never achieve the effectiveness of an entrepreneurial conversation.

The most masterful entrepreneurial conversations result in specific plans for action such as "who will do what by when." Creating detailed assignments for everyone encourages participants to be accountable for the actions and results they agreed would be their responsibilities.

Identify the Best Possibility

Research has shown that a pause to "sleep on" a list of possibilities allows ideas to percolate and new concepts to evolve. Recent studies have produced evidence that even dreaming at night can be an effective way for people to find solutions by opening up different thinking patterns.

After you "sleep on" your list of possibilities, meet again and rank all the ideas in order of their attractiveness. Ideas don't get discarded...only ranked from most appealing to least appealing. Leave yourself open to mixing and matching characteristics of various ideas to create a winning course of action.

Overcoming Rejection

Mastering the entrepreneurial conversation will greatly reduce the amount of rejection you will endure since you and the other person will be exploring possibilities for working together. Entrepreneurial conversations are about doing research first and then developing ideas with people who can benefit from them. You are not presenting your ideas for the other person to either accept or reject.

However, there will always be times when you realize that a working relationship will not be likely. Your service might not accomplish what the other person needs, or he may already be satisfied with a competitor's product.

For rejections that can't be avoided, the key is not to perceive them as personal criticisms. If you're talking with other people about a product, investment or job that is not right for them—or for you—then you are not having an entrepreneurial conversation and you are giving them a reason to reject you. Otherwise, you need to evaluate the situation and make certain you're not misinterpreting some aspect of the conversation, especially nonverbal cues.

Think back to the scene we set in *Chapter 3: Listen Like a Successful Entrepreneur* regarding the recent MBA graduates whose cockiness may be off-putting. If these types of interactions intimidate you or make you feel less well-educated because you don't have an advanced degree, you may miss out on a wonderful opportunity to work with bright, enthusiastic funders. Try to look at each situation honestly and without prejudice to make certain you're not misinterpreting the message you may think is being sent.

Underneath all the emotional baggage connected with rejection, it is nothing more than a decision not to accept an offer to work together. It's that simple, and it's almost never personal. It's best for you to accept the decision and go home to reevaluate your product or service and the interest of the people you intend to contact in the future.

If you do determine that the decision to not work together is personal—that the other person is so prejudiced she can't work with someone with blue eyes—then chalk it up to her limitations, not yours, and move on to another potential working relationship.

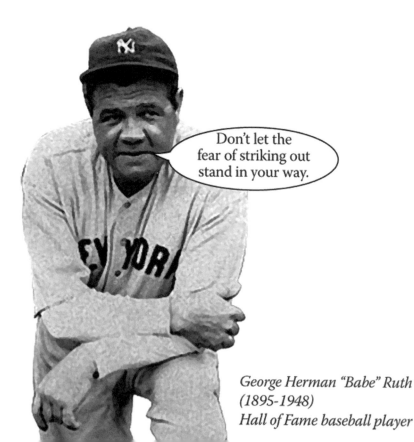

George Herman "Babe" Ruth
(1895-1948)
Hall of Fame baseball player

Don't Be Misled

If you're an entrepreneur, beware of certain funding sources, such as venture capital firms, which are proposal-friendly and may give you the wrong impression about their eagerness. Some investors don't want to develop a reputation for not doing deals, so they encourage a constant flow of proposals across their desks. They may withhold sharing their exact investment guidelines with potential clients in order to keep those submissions coming.

If you're a salesperson and you believe an old-school boss who encourages you to make proposals to everyone and anyone, you will encounter a great deal of rejection. Barking up the wrong tree is a waste of your time and certainly doesn't convince the tree to do anything.

The plus of this system is that these investors will look at any plan or project that's submitted. The minus is that you will never learn exactly why they turned down your deal—and you won't know how to improve your approach to other potential investors in the future.

In an entrepreneurial conversation, you form the ideas and proposals jointly with the other person. You are not simply asking the other person to buy, invest, or take the job being offered. You are discussing the possibility of working together for mutual benefit. Keeping that goal in mind will drastically reduce the number of times you are rejected or even feel rejected.

Follow the Network

The entrepreneurial conversation is a powerful tool in virtually any business setting, but it's even more effective when you're talking to people who are open to new ideas. Clients, colleagues, employees and investors who are willing to try new solutions, products and concepts, subsequently communicate what they've learned along their extensive networks. And *their* networks will benefit *your* networks.

The best people to contact are what publishing consultant Mike Shatzkin calls "megaphones." They are the bright, independent and ambitious thinkers who want to share their ideas and enthusiasm with others. "Megaphones" are important to entrepreneurial people who are looking for good clients, colleagues, investors or employees.

"Megaphones" are far more willing than others in their fields to adopt innovations. Everett M. Rogers, a professor of communications and journalism at the University of New Mexico, has devoted his professional life to analyzing the process of how innovations are adopted. In *Diffusion of Innovations*, Rogers identifies the significant role networks play in influencing people. The acceptance of a new product or service is largely determined by whether leaders, or what he terms "early adopters," begin to use the innovation. Rogers shows how these networks of people represent the paths along which changes move from person to person, with the same early adopters remaining the leaders.

Rogers describes a vivid example of this phenomenon in a 1966 study on how doctors adopted the antibiotic tetracycline in their practices. The top determinant of which doctors began to prescribe the drug was how much contact they had with other doctors, including affiliation with a hospital, practicing in a group, and having other physicians as friends. After ten months, virtually all the doctors with a great deal of contact with other physicians were prescribing tetracycline, while only half of those with little contact with other doctors had adopted the drug.

Rogers' research identifies how early adopters stand out from others in their fields by being:

- More empathetic
- More adaptable and flexible
- More able to think abstractly
- More able to think independently
- More rational
- More intelligent
- More favorable toward change
- More able to cope with uncertainty
- More accepting of science
- More affluent
- More in control of their lives
- More ambitious
- More socially active
- More highly educated

Because early adopters are key to the process of spreading innovations, and because they are better connected to professional and social networks, they make excellent contacts for entrepreneurial people in any field. Since early adopters are eager to find new solutions to problems, prefer to be stimulated creatively and have the financial security to risk trying new ideas, they can readily be engaged in entrepreneurial conversations.

The Critical Value of Referrals

No matter what career you have chosen, referrals will be crucial in helping you find early adopters who can become your clients, colleagues, investors and employees.

Entrepreneurs with noncompetitive products that do business with the same industries can be a valuable source of referrals that you may have overlooked. Equipment buyers for hospitals deal with dozens of salespeople, many of whom are selling product lines that don't compete with each other, such as wheelchairs and linen services. If you and an entrepreneur with a non-competing company can introduce each other to buyers with whom you each do business, you can increase the size of your network.

A study by Sarah Lorge, a writer for *Sales and Marketing Management,* found that 80 percent of all clients would be happy to provide referrals to salespeople who called on them, but only 20 percent were asked to do so. Lorge also discovered that referrals were twelve times more likely to lead to a business relationship than cold calls.

Funding sources sometimes will reject your proposal simply because it doesn't fit their interests, not because it's a bad proposal. They are often willing to pass proposals along to colleagues at other firms, or will allow you to use their names when you call their contacts.

Wisdom
of the
Entrepreneurial
Masters
Chauncey Rapp

Chauncey Rapp is a perfect example of someone who has mastered the art of the entrepreneurial conversation. Chauncey was born into the printing business. His father, a Russian immigrant, became a printer in 1920, and went on to build his own substantial printing business.

When Chauncey graduated from Carnegie Tech (now Carnegie Mellon University) in 1947, he joined his father's business as an estimator, until a salesman retired and his customer list became available. For the next fifty years, first with his father's company, and later with his own firm, Chauncey sold printing services to publishers, advertising agencies and other corporate accounts.

"I'm not a glad-hander and I don't have a gift of gab," Chauncey says. "I had the knowledge of my business and was able to solve problems for clients; therefore, I could build rapport and trust with them. Some clients hired printing firms based solely on the lowest bidder. The key to getting those jobs was figuring out ways to meet the client's needs inexpensively. Other jobs were not based solely on price, but on having rapport and trust with the client."

"I also relied on networking," Chauncey says. "My paper suppliers had other clients who needed good printers, so we shared customer names and I built my client base faster than I expected. There was this young Russian immigrant who had worked for me and went out on his own to start a specialized printing service that didn't compete with mine. I remembered my father and his struggles to get started, so I referred my clients to the new guy if he could do the job better. I learned that doing best by the client worked out best for everyone in the long run."

"I didn't lie to clients or try to oversell," continues Chauncey. "Once, a production manager for a major publisher asked me if my company could reshoot the negatives for a job they were doing. I looked at the negatives they already had and told him that they looked pretty good and I didn't think we could do better. The production manager said, 'That's exactly what I've been telling the people around here.' After that, I was really in-like-Flynn with him."

"Salesmen are middlemen," says Chauncey. "The ones who socialized with clients but didn't have product knowledge would introduce the client to the printer's production manager to work out the job. I preferred to work out more of the details myself. Really, no matter what you do in business," adds Chauncey, "you are selling. Everyone who is successful in business can sell. But if a publisher was always late with payments and messed up my ability to pay my vendors, I didn't keep working with them. It wasn't worth my time. I guess I thought of all my clients more like my partners. We had to work together to get a job done."

Chauncey's success is a perfect example of how to use the entrepreneurial conversation to reach your business goals. He always focused on the real issues and made sure that he was working to meet his clients' needs. Chauncey built long-term relationships with his clients, but was willing to end relationships that were going nowhere. Finally, he maximized the value of his networks by relying on referrals, helping other people in the industry, and building a reputation for honesty and superior results. "There was no secret to my success," Chauncey says, "I knew my product and used my knowledge to meet customers' needs."

One Final Word to Our Readers

Now that you've finished the book, we hope that your ability to engage in entrepreneurial conversations is well established. But remember that mastery is an ongoing process. Stay alert, be open-minded, keep learning from others and, above all, think, listen and speak like a successful entrepreneur.

Index